THE
PRECAUTIONARY
PRINCIPLE

THE
PRECAUTIONARY PRINCIPLE

A Critical Appraisal of Environmental Risk Assessment

Indur M. Goklany

INSTITUTE
Washington, D.C.

Library of Congress Cataloging-in-Publication Data

Goklany, Indur M.
  The precautionary principle : a critical appraisal of environment
risk assessment / Indur M. Goklany.
    p. cm.
  Includes bibliographical references and index.
  ISBN 1-930865-16-3
  1. Environmental risk assessment. I. Title.
  GE145 .G64 2001
  363.7'02–dc21

                                                          2001047310
Cover design by Elise Rivera.

Printed in the United States of America.

CATO INSTITUTE
1000 Massachusetts Ave., N.W.
Washington, D.C. 2001

Contents

Acknowledgments

I was fortunate to have support and encouragement from several quarters while writing this book. In particular, I thank Julian Morris for helping me embark on and persist in this endeavor. The book originated as a chapter in his fine book, *Rethinking Risk and the Precautionary Principle* (Oxford: Butterworth Heinemann, 2000). I also thank Roger Bate, Ken Chilton, and Don Roberts for their detailed reviews and comments on earlier versions of various chapters in my book. I wrote parts of the book in the summer of 2000 while I was the D&D Foundation Julian Simon Fellow at the Political Economy Research Center in Bozeman, Montana. I am grateful to Terry Anderson, Rich Stroup, Jane Shaw, Roger Meiners, P.J. Hill, Dan Benjamin, Roger Sedjo, Don Leal, and the entire PERC crew for their company and support during my tenure there. I was doubly fortunate in Bozeman to be the guest of Juliette Shaw and Eric Noyes, and the Meiners family. This book, moreover, would not have been published without the support of the Cato Institute's Jerry Taylor, David Boaz, and David Lampo.

Thanks to Ken Chilton, previous versions of the biotechnology and global warming chapters of this book appeared as policy studies from the Center for the Study of American Business (now the Weidenbaum Center), Washington University in St. Louis. A version of the former also appeared in the *Biotechnology Law Report*. The DDT chapter was published on the "Save Children from Malaria Campaign" Web site, courtesy of Roger Bate and Kendra Okonski.

And, of course, no such undertaking can ever be successful without constant support and encouragement from the home front. To Maya, Sam, and, especially, Karen, I dedicate this book.

1. Escaping Goblins, Only to Be Captured by Wolves?

"What shall we do, what shall we do!" he cried. "Escaping goblins to be caught by wolves!"

—J. R. R. Tolkien, *The Hobbit*, p. 98

So what do we do if we come to a fork in the road and one way leads through territory inhabited by goblins and the other through country infested by wolves? Which road should we take? Does it even matter if we take one road and not the other?

Policymakers in the environmental and public health arena often face such dilemmas. DDT (dichlorodiphenyltrichloroethane) is a classic case. On one hand, this much-reviled chemical is a proven, cheap, and effective method of reducing malaria, a disease that annually afflicts 300 million people and claims over a million lives worldwide (WHO 2000). Over the years, DDT has saved millions of lives not only in Asia and Africa but also in Europe and the Americas. But DDT has also been implicated in the decline of a number of raptors such as the bald eagle and the peregrine falcon. It has been found in various avian eggshells, in the tissues of fish, and in mothers' milk. Some suspect it plays a role in advancing various human cancers and other disorders (Roberts 1999, Attaran et al. 2000, Tren and Bate 2001).

So what should be the policy toward DDT? Should it be banned because of its effects on birds and its hypothesized adverse public health effects? Should its use be encouraged because of its proven ability to combat malaria, one of nature's dread diseases? Or should different policies prevail in different areas, depending on whether those areas are plagued by malaria or host species that might be threatened by DDT?

Today's environmentalists have increasingly invoked the precautionary principle to solve such policy dilemmas. This principle is, essentially, a restatement of a popular rendition of the Hippocratic

1

oath, namely, "first do no harm." Its advocates would have it become a cornerstone for developing policies related to the environment and public health (e.g., Raffensperger and Tickner 1999: 1, 22, 334).

Based on the precautionary principle, many environmentalists have supported a global ban on DDT, arguing that, by endangering various avian species, it would harm the environment and that it might possibly contribute to various health problems in human beings. But might not such a ban itself harm public health and result in a higher death toll by postponing, if not foregoing, the conquest of malaria in several developing countries? How do we resolve this dilemma?

This book concerns itself with how the precautionary principle could be used to solve various public health and environmental dilemmas, and to ensure that policies to address them do not ultimately cause more harm than good. In this context, it will, as case examples, apply the principle to various policies related to DDT, genetically modified crops, and global warming.

The Precautionary Principle

A popular and reasonably good definition of the precautionary principle can be found in the so-called Wingspread Declaration (Raffensperger and Tickner 1999: 8):

> When an activity raises threats of harm to human health or the environment, precautionary measures should be taken even if some cause and effect relationships are not established scientifically.
> In this context the proponent of the activity, rather than the public, should bear the burden of proof.

Many people—environmentalists and others—interpret this principle to imply that if there are any doubts about the safety of a technology, that technology ought to be severely restricted if not banned, unless it can be proven to be absolutely safe (Tickner 1999: 168–169; see, e.g., Stone 2001). In this vein, Greenpeace's Leggett stated, "The modus operandi we would like to see is: 'Do not emit a substance unless you have proof it will do no harm to the environment'" (Leggett 1990: 459; see also Jordan and O'Riordan 1999: 25). Such "absolutist" interpretations capture well the skepticism with which many environmentalists regard technology in general (see, e.g., Goklany 1996).

Others, noting that there can never be absolute certainty or absolute safety, argue that it is irrational to apply the precautionary principle to policymaking in a world where resources—fiscal and human—are scarce, and that the principle might be counterproductive because it would reduce technological progress toward risk reduction (e.g., Cross 1996, Morris 2000, Stone 2001). Technological progress, the critics argue, is the time-tested method for reducing society's vulnerability to all kinds of adversity (Goklany 1992, 1995a, 2000a). For instance, until this century, the major health risks to humanity included inadequate supplies of food; poor access to safe water and sanitation; and insufficient knowledge of basic hygiene, the germ theory, and infectious and vector-borne diseases. Today, because of technological progress in the last century and a half, those risks have been significantly reduced in the developing—and virtually eliminated in the developed—world (Goklany 1999a, 2001a). As a result, life expectancy, perhaps the single most critical indicator of human well-being, has more than doubled in that period.

Instead of joining the debate regarding the rationality of the precautionary principle and taking sides, I will assume that it is indeed a viable approach to policymaking. And although one must agree with law professor Christopher Stone (2001: 24) that the precautionary principle is not "entrenched in customary law," variations of it can be found in at least 14 international environmental declarations, agreements, and conventions (Stone 2001: note 1). In this book, I take the principle as given and use it to evaluate and develop policies with respect to the specific environmental issues of DDT, genetically modified crops, and global warming.

Origins of the Principle

While the eminent legal scholar Frank Cross claims that the phrase "precautionary principle" was coined by German bureaucrats in 1965, other scholars (Morris 2000) claim that it derives from the 1970s and the German articulation of *Vorsorgeprinzip*, which can be translated as the "precaution" or "foresight" principle. But its roots go deeper. They extend at least to the very first mother who admonished her child that it is "better to be safe than sorry" (see, e.g., Cross 1996, Adler 2000).

The spirit of the precautionary principle can be found in several U.S. laws enacted before the principle acquired international fame, if not its name. The Delaney Clause, which was included in Section 409 of the U.S. Federal Food, Drug and Cosmetic Act of 1958, for instance, essentially outlawed any food additive that was found to induce cancer in real life or in laboratory tests on animals (Vogt 1995), regardless of the magnitude of the dose. This is perhaps the apotheosis of the absolutist version of the precautionary principle. It can also be argued that the 1970 Clean Air Act effectively operationalized the absolutist version of the precautionary principle. The Act required not only that primary (that is, public health–related) National Ambient Air Quality Standards be established without consideration of social or economic costs (Cross 1996: 856), but also that all states meet the standards by a date certain, regardless of the difficulties or costs of meeting standards.

Various versions of the precautionary principle started to appear in international environmental declarations and agreements in the 1980s. Championed by environmentalists and European governments eager to garnish their green stripes, the principle started appearing in one environmental forum after another. It seems to have made its international debut in 1982 in the United Nations World Charter for Nature, which stated that when "potential adverse effects [of activities likely to pose significant risks to nature] are not fully understood, the activities should not proceed" (Cross 1996, Stone 2001). In 1987 it appeared in the Second International Conference on the Protection of the North Sea (e.g., Morris 2000: 3). By the late 1980s and early 1990s, discussions of the precautionary principle or precautionary approach were a staple of international environmental discussions. In 1990 alone, "precautionary" language was, for instance, included in the Final Declaration of the Third International Conference on the Protection of the North Sea (in March), the Bergen Ministerial Declaration at a Conference on Sustainable Development of the U.N. Economic Conference for Europe (in May), and the Second World Climate Conference (in December) (Morris 2000: 4–5; Raffensperger and Tickner 1999: 356–61).

Variations on the Precautionary Theme

By the time the United Nations Conference on Environment and Development (UNCED) met in Rio de Janeiro in 1992, the precautionary principle was well-nigh ubiquitous. At UNCED, somewhat

4

different versions of it were incorporated in the Rio Declaration on Environment and Development, the United Nations Framework Convention on Climate Change, and the Convention on Biological Diversity.

Principle 15 of the Rio Declaration (UN 1992: 10) proclaimed, for instance,

> In order to protect the environment, the precautionary approach shall be widely applied by States according to their capabilities. Where there are threats of serious or irreversible damage, lack of full scientific certainty shall not be used as a reason for postponing cost-effective measures to prevent environmental degradation.

The first sentence of this version, by implying that states may constrain their application "according to their capabilities" and that it "shall be *widely* applied" (italics are mine), seems to envision some flexibility and a less-than-absolutist application of the principle. The next sentence is even more tentative. It may be argued that its first part is essentially vacuous, since we can almost never have "full scientific certainty" (Cross 1996: note 10), and therefore—like it or not—actions are almost invariably taken "in the absence of full scientific certainty." This sentence does not require any specific type of action on the part of a state, and it implies that actions that are not "cost-effective" need not be taken. Thus, Principle 15 of the Rio Declaration is not as sweeping as either the Wingspread Declaration or the absolutist interpretation of the precautionary principle requiring limits on any technology unless proven absolutely safe.

Principle 15 is echoed in the Preamble of the Convention on Biological Diversity (CBD) with the exception that it eschews any reference to cost-effectiveness. The precautionary principle included in that Convention (Glowka et al. 1994: 11) states as follows:

> That it is vital to anticipate, prevent and attack the causes of significant reduction or loss of biological diversity at source,. . .
> Where there is a threat of significant reduction or loss of biological diversity, lack of full scientific certainty should not be used as a reason for postponing measures to avoid or minimize such a threat.

However, although lack of full scientific certainty may not be used to postpone measures, this version does not preclude rejecting actions that might be economically inefficient (or not cost-effective).

The version of the precautionary principle articulated in Article 3.3 of the U.N. Framework Convention on Climate Change (UNFCCC),

5

although more forthright, is much less absolutist. Like to the CBD version, it commences by explicitly stating that "the Parties should take precautionary measures to anticipate, prevent or minimize the causes of climate change and mitigate its adverse effects" (UNFCCC 1992). Notably it uses "should" rather than "must." It is similar in a number of other ways to Principle 15, with one critical difference. Specifically, Article 3.3 goes on to state as follows:

> Where there are threats of serious or irreversible damage, lack of full scientific certainty should not be used as a reason for postponing such measures, taking into account that policies and measures to deal with climate change should be cost-effective so as to ensure global benefits at the lowest possible cost. To achieve this, such policies and measures should take into account different socio/economic contexts, be comprehensive, cover all relevant sources, sinks and reservoirs of greenhouse gases and adaptation, and comprise all economic sectors.

This version, unlike the other versions encountered previously, specifies that climate change policies and measures "should" essentially be based on global cost-benefit analyses. However, many commentators have—conveniently or otherwise—overlooked this requirement in the UNFCCC for the design of climate change related policies (IPCC 1996a: 5; Goklany 2000b). But if, and only if, one overlooks this inconvenient detail does the UNFCCC seem consistent with the absolutist interpretation of the Wingspread Declaration.

Out of these various versions of the precautionary principle eventually emerged, in January 2000, the Cartagena Protocol on Biosafety to the Convention on Biological Diversity, which repeatedly uses the precautionary principle as a basis for decisionmaking and risk assessment with respect to the transboundary transfer (and associated handling and use) of genetically modified organisms that may have adverse effects on the conservation and sustainable use of biological diversity (CBD 2000). Rightly or wrongly, as Frances Smith (2000) has noted, the Cartagena Protocol is seen as a major victory for the more absolutist version of the precautionary principle and for its advocates.

A Double-Edged Sword

In keeping with its origins in technological skepticism, the precautionary principle has also been increasingly invoked as justification, among other things, for international controls, if not outright bans, on various technologies, which—despite providing substantial benefits to humanity and, in some cases, to certain aspects of the environment—could also worsen other aspects of the environment or public health (Goklany 2000c). In addition to DDT, other technologies against which the principle has been invoked are fossil fuel combustion, on which much of the world's current prosperity and human well-being are based but which could help cause catastrophic global warming (Goklany 1999a, 2001a), and genetically modified crops, which promise to reduce global hunger and malnutrition while making agriculture more environmentally sustainable but which have also raised the specter of "frankenfoods" and "super-weeds" (FOE 1999a; Goklany 2000c, 2001b).

The justifications for these policies have something more than the precautionary principle in common: They also share a common flaw. Each of these justifications takes credit for the public health and environmental risks that might be reduced by implementing the policy, but they overlook those public health and environmental risks that the policy itself might generate or prolong. As a result, these policy prescriptions could be worse for humanity and the environment than the underlying diseases they seek to redress (Cross 1996, Adler 2000, Comstock 2000, Goklany 2000c, Goklany et al. 2001). In essence, we might escape the goblins but be crushed by the jaws of wolves.

A one-sided application of the precautionary principle leads to such a predicament because the principle itself provides no guidance on its application in situations where an action (such as a ban on GM crops) could simultaneously lead to uncertain benefits and uncertain harms (Goklany 2000d). In this regard, the principle is reminiscent of Yogi Berra's admonition, "When you come to a fork in the road, take it."

So what do we do to ensure that in avoiding goblins we do not fall prey to wolves?

It is important to ensure that precautionary policies are not counterproductive for public health and the environment. In the following section, I will develop a framework for applying the precautionary principle in situations in which outcomes might be ambiguous because their benefits might be partly or wholly offset by their harms. The framework is developed with reference to the version of the precautionary principle articulated by the Wingspread Declaration. This framework is applied in subsequent chapters to evaluate whether various environmental policies touted as precautionary would in fact reduce overall risks to public health and the environment. And if they do not, this book presents alternative policies that, indeed, will.

In Chapter 2, I use the framework to evaluate whether a worldwide ban on DDT would, in fact, improve public health and reduce environmental risks worldwide. That chapter also addresses whether the precautionary principle demands a one-size-fits-all approach toward DDT, with identical requirements for developed and developing countries, and whether a DDT phase-out by a date certain is necessarily consistent with the principle. In Chapter 2, I also discuss whether, given the potential benefits of using DDT indoors for public health in malaria-prone developing countries, and the quarter-century-long declining trends in environmental concentrations of DDT worldwide, international regulation of DDT is warranted.

Chapter 3 applies the framework to determine whether an unbiased and comprehensive application of the precautionary principle would justify banning GM crops. It also examines whether such a ban would be consistent with, or further the stated aims and objectives of, the international Convention on Biological Diversity, the Cartagena Biosafety Protocol, and various international declarations that might be read to imply that freedom from hunger and malnutrition is a fundamental human right. Chapter 3 also addresses other arguments that have been offered as rationales for a GM crop ban, namely, that the rich OECD nations are "awash in surplus grain," they do not need to increase either food production or productivity, and that the world's real problems are unequal access and maldistribution rather than insufficient food.

Chapter 4 examines the policy of forcing the pace of greenhouse gas reductions beyond what would occur with secular (i.e., "normal") trends in technological change. It also addresses the role of adaptation as a precautionary policy in relation to climate change.

A Framework for Applying the Precautionary Principle under Competing Uncertainties

Few actions are either unmitigated disasters or unadulterated benefits, and certainty in science is the exception rather than the rule.

How, then, do we formulate precautionary policies in situations where an action could lead simultaneously to uncertain benefits and uncertain harms (or costs) to public health and the environment?

The only way to implement the precautionary principle intelligently under such conditions is to formulate hierarchical criteria and rank various threats based upon their characteristics and the degree of certainty attached to them. Consequently, I offer a set of criteria to construct a precautionary framework.

The first of these is the *human mortality criterion*—that is, the threat of death to any human being, no matter how lowly that human being may be, outweighs similar threats to members of other species, no matter how magnificent those species. Moreover, in general, other nonmortal threats to human health should take precedence over threats to the environment, although there might be exceptions based on the nature, severity, and extent of the threat. I will call this the *human morbidity criterion*. These two criteria can be combined into the *public health criterion*.

However, when an action under consideration results in both potential benefits and potential harms to public health, additional criteria have to be brought into play. These additional criteria are also valid for cases in which the action under consideration results in positive as well as negative environmental impacts unrelated to public health. I propose five such criteria:

- The *immediacy criterion*. All else being equal, more immediate threats should be given priority over threats that could occur later. Support for this criterion can be found in the fact that people tend to partially discount the value of human lives that might be lost in the more distant future (Cropper and Portney 1992). Although some may question whether such discounting is ethical, it may be justified on the grounds that if death does not come immediately, with greater knowledge and new technology methods may be found in the future to deal with conditions that would otherwise be fatal, and that, in turn, may postpone death even longer. For instance, between 1995 and 1999, estimated AIDS-related deaths in the United States dropped by over two-thirds (from 50,610 to 16,273) even though estimated cases increased by almost half (from 216,796 to 320,282) (CDC 2000a: Tables 23 and 26). Thus, if an HIV-positive person in the United States did not succumb to AIDS by 1998 because of advances in medicine, there was a greater likelihood in 1998 that he would live out his normal life span. Accordingly, it would be reasonable to give greater weight to premature deaths that occur sooner. This is related to, but distinct from, the *adaptation criterion* noted below.

- The *uncertainty criterion*. Threats of harm that are more certain (have higher probabilities of occurrence) should take precedence over those that are less certain if their consequences otherwise would be equivalent. (I do not examine in this book how equivalency should be determined for different kinds of threats.)
- The *expectation-value criterion*. For threats that are equally certain, precedence should be given to those that have a higher expectation value. An action resulting in fewer expected deaths is preferred over one that would result in a larger number of expected deaths (assuming that the "quality of lives saved" is equivalent). Similarly, if an action poses a greater risk to biodiversity than inaction, the latter ought to be favored.
- The *adaptation criterion*. If technologies are available to cope with, or adapt to, the adverse consequences of an impact, then that impact can be discounted to the extent that the threat can be nullified.
- The *irreversibility criterion*. Greater priority should be given to outcomes that are irreversible, or likely to be more persistent.

Ideally, each criterion would be applied, one at a time, to the various sets of public health and environmental consequences of the action under review (minus, for each category, the consequences of persisting with the status quo, or whatever the other options might be). Such an approach could work relatively easily if the factors critical to each criterion were kept constant, except the ones related to the criterion under evaluation. But, because the various factors are rarely equal, the net effects (on each of the sets of consequences) usually have to be evaluated by applying several of the criteria simultaneously.

If the results are equivocal with respect to the different sets of consequences, one should apply the human mortality and morbidity criteria. For example, if the action might directly or indirectly increase net human mortality but improve the environment by increasing the recreational potential of a water body, then the action ought to be rejected.

There will obviously be instances in which no cut-and-dried answer is readily apparent. For example, an action might reduce cases of a nonlethal human disease while at the same time potentially killing a large number of animals. In such cases, in addition to considering factors such as the nature, severity, and curability of the disease, the cost of the disease and/or treatment, and the numbers of human and other species affected (factors subsumed in the previously specified criteria, namely, the adaptation, irreversibility, and expectation value criteria), decisionmaking should also consider factors such as the abundance of the species and whether the species is threatened or endangered.

2. DDT: Silent Spring or Silent People?

Dichlorodiphenyltrichloroethane (DDT) has a remarkable and checkered history. Once a boon to mankind, it is now considered by many to be a bane to the environment.

DDT was first synthesized in 1874 by Othmar Zeidler in Strasbourg, Germany, but it was another six decades before its remarkable insecticidal properties were discovered by Paul Mueller in Switzerland (*Encyclopedia Britannica* 1959: vol. 14, 706A; vol. 15, 939). It was first used to control typhus from lice in 1942. Shortly thereafter, the U.S. Department of Agriculture found it was an efficient exterminator of mosquitoes, flies, fleas, and other insects. Thus began its use not only as a malaria control agent but also as an agricultural insecticide.

In the early 1940s, when the world's population was less than half of what it is today, it was estimated that malaria, a mosquito-borne disease suspected to have plagued humanity since prehistoric times, afflicted at least 300 million people worldwide, causing 3 million deaths annually including over 1 million in India alone (*Encyclopedia Britannica* 1959: vol. 14, 706A). With the help of DDT, the global malaria death rate—which had been 1,740 per million in 1930—dropped over 70 percent to 480 per million in 1950 (WHO 1999a).

In recognition of DDT's role in the remarkable progress against this ancient disease, Paul Mueller was awarded the Nobel Prize for Physiology and Medicine in 1948. By 1970 the global malaria death rate, had dropped another two-thirds to 160 per million (WHO 1999a). Malaria had been virtually eliminated in the developed world and was on the wane in much of the rest of the world, except for Sub-Saharan Africa (WHO 1999a: 50).

But in the meantime, the dark side of DDT had been discovered. First, some mosquitoes developed resistance to DDT (*Encyclopedia Britannica* 1959: vol. 14, 706A), probably because of DDT's massive use as an agricultural pesticide (Meiners and Morriss 2001). In the 1950s DDT was detected in mothers' milk. It was also associated with the thinning of eggshells and declining populations of various raptor species, such as bald eagles (WWF 1999).

13

In 1962, Rachel Carson's brilliant and lyrical polemic *Silent Spring* marshaled the environmental case against DDT and other pesticides. By that time malaria was a fast-fading memory in the developed world. In fact, in the developed countries the paramount health-related issue regarding DDT seems to have been its potential carcinogenicity rather than its remarkable success in limiting malaria (EDF 1972). Soon some developed nations began banning its use and production within their own borders. In a move celebrated by many environmentalists as one of the 20th century's greatest environmental victories, Administrator Ruckelshaus of the Environmental Protection Agency banned DDT use in the United States in 1972 (EDF 1972, Lazaroff 1999).

However, many environmental groups were not about to rest on their laurels. Alarmed by reports that DDT and its various metabolites (i.e., products formed during its breakdown) were being detected in mothers' milk, fatty tissues of various species, and on the surface in places as remote as the Arctic Circle, and concerned about their bioaccumulative properties and any associated potential public health and environmental consequences, environmentalists succeeded in getting some of the more developed countries to support an eventual global ban on DDT (WWF 1999, PSR 1999). And despite the fact that malaria had staged a comeback in many parts of the developing world, an international agreement with the stated goal of phasing out DDT use worldwide was reached in December 2000 under the auspices of the United Nations Environmental Programme. But, in a compromise with developing countries where DDT is still used to control endemic malaria, the phaseout was postponed until cost-effective and environmentally friendly alternatives become available (UNEP 2000).

The rationale offered for a global DDT ban is that the precautionary principle requires it (WWF 1999). However, whereas such a ban might eliminate any potential public health and environmental problems associated with DDT use, it might also aggravate or prolong malaria problems in areas where that disease still persists.

This chapter applies the framework developed in the last chapter to evaluate whether a global DDT ban would indeed be consistent with the precautionary principle and whether that would make for a sound global policy for minimizing overall public health and environmental risks. In case it does not, I propose alternatives that might.

The Public Health Risks of Banning DDT

Whether a ban on DDT adds to the public health risk in an area depends on whether or not malaria is prevalent there. The global death rate due to malaria was 18 per 100,000 in 1998, down from 194 per 100,000 in 1900 (WHO 1999a). This more than 10-fold reduction is due to better nutrition, new drugs, draining and filling of wetlands (swamps and marshes), insecticide-impregnated mosquito nets, and spraying of insecticides (particularly DDT) inside homes. Yet, each year 1.1 million people die from malaria (WHO 2000). The vast majority of the death toll occurs in developing countries because malaria—thanks partly to DDT—has, for practical purposes, been almost completely eradicated in the developed world.

There is good evidence that, despite the buildup of mosquito resistance to DDT, the global death toll would be higher if in-home spraying of DDT where malaria is currently endemic were to be discontinued. First, DDT combats malaria through three mechanisms: repellency, irritability, and toxicity. (Attaran et al. 2000). Studies find that indoor DDT spraying repels mosquitoes, and significantly fewer mosquitoes venture into houses that have been sprayed with DDT. In a study by Grieco et al. (2000), 97 percent fewer mosquitoes entered DDT-sprayed huts than entered unsprayed huts. By contrast, 66 percent fewer mosquitoes entered huts sprayed with deltamethrin, a pyrethroid touted as a substitute for DDT (Raloff 2000). In other words, 11 times as many mosquitoes entered the deltamethrin-sprayed hut as entered the DDT-sprayed hut. This suggests that if in the long run mosquitoes develop resistance to both DDT and deltamethrin, DDT is likely to be more effective in controlling malaria.

If, despite DDT's repellency, mosquitoes come into contact with DDT, it acts as an irritant that drives them away, sometimes even before they bite (Raloff 2000). And if they are not driven away, DDT's toxicity can kill them. Developing resistance only affects the last of these mechanisms. Based on a probability model of mosquito behavior, Roberts et al. (2000a) suggest that the combined effect of DDT repellency and irritability dominates over its toxicity in reducing malaria. According to their model, toxicity accounted for less than 10 percent of DDT's effectiveness for three species—*Anopheles darlingi* (Ituxi River), and *A. gambiae* (Tanzania), *A. punctulatus* (Irian Jaya)—less than 40 percent for *A. darlingi* (Suriname), and less than 20 percent for *A. funestus* (Tanzania).

The first two mechanisms (i.e., repellency and irritancy) for reducing exposure to carriers of malaria parasites are important for another reason: Some species are becoming resistant to some of the pesticides used as DDT substitutes. For example, *A. funestus* in South Africa seems to have increased resistance to pyrethroids (Raloff 2000, Bate 2000). Resistance to DDT is still limited to certain species of anopheles mosquitoes in some locations (Roberts et al. 2000b, Bate 2000).

More importantly, alternatives to DDT, even if they are available, do not necessarily lead to equivalent reductions in malaria incidence if the alternatives are more expensive because cost is an important factor in developing countries. Attaran et al. (2000) note that if India switched from DDT to malathion, the next cheapest option, the number of people at high risk of contracting malaria would increase by 71 million (equivalent to 25 percent of the U.S. population), assuming level funding. Raloff (2000) reported that deltamethrin, which costs three to four times as much as DDT, now consumes 89 percent of Belize's malaria control budget, which starves funds from surveillance, elimination of mosquito breeding grounds, and even malaria treatment.

The additional cost may seem trivial to inhabitants of the developed countries, but it is very significant in developing countries, where the average household spends more than 50 percent of its income for the most basic of necessities—food (Meade and Rosen 1996). For instance, the average Nepalese family, with a per capita income of $220 per year [at market exchange rates (World Bank 2000)], spends 63 percent of its budget on food (*Kathmandu Post* 2000). That means very little is left over for other basic necessities such as shelter, clothing, education, and health. In India, for instance, the average per capita health expenditure is $10 per year (McNeil 2000)—the price in the United States of less than half a year's supply of vitamin supplements. Of that $10, $3.50 is spent on drugs (McNeil 2000). Not surprisingly, governments in developing countries have to weigh costs and cost-effectiveness carefully before selecting the types and extent of public health measures that they implement.

Given the greater efficacy of DDT and the higher costs of alternatives, it is not surprising that despite the theoretical availability of substitutes, malaria rebounded in many poor areas where (and when) DDT use was discontinued (WHO 1999a, Roberts 1999,

Roberts et al. 1997, Sharma 1996, Whelan 1992, Guarda et al. 1999, Bate 2000). For instance, the incidence of malaria in Sri Lanka (Ceylon) dropped from 2.8 million in the 1940s to less than 20 in 1963 (WHO 1999a, Whelan 1992). DDT spraying was stopped there in 1964, and by 1969 the number of cases had grown to 2.5 million. In India malaria was nearly eradicated in the early 1960s, and its resurgence coincided with shortages of DDT (Sharma 1996). The population at high to medium risk of contracting malaria in Colombia and Peru doubled between 1996 and 1997 (Roberts et al. 2000b).

Malaria has also reappeared in several other areas where it had previously been suppressed, if not eradicated—for example, Madagascar, Swaziland, the two Koreas, Armenia, Azerbaijan, Turkmenistan (Roberts et al. 2000b and references therein). Roberts et al. (1997) show that in Latin American countries such as Ecuador, Belize, Guyana, Bolivia, Paraguay, Brazil, and Venezuela, which had discontinued or decreased spraying of DDT inside homes, malaria rates increased. Guarda et al. (1999) note that in 1988, when DDT use was discontinued, there were no reported cases of *Plasmodium falciparum* in Loreto, Peru. The number of cases increased to 140 in 1991. By 1997, there were more than 54,000 cases and 85 deaths (see also, Goklany 2000c).

But the best argument for indoor spraying of DDT is that in many areas where malaria experienced a resurgence, resuming DDT use once again led to declines in malaria cases. For example, in Ecuador, where malaria rates rebounded after DDT spraying was reduced, those rates have declined once again—by 61 percent since 1993, when DDT use again increased (Roberts et al. 1997). The same cycle occurred in Madagascar, where the malaria epidemic of 1984–86, which occurred after the suspension of DDT use, killed 100,000 people. After two annual cycles of DDT spraying, malaria incidence declined by 90 percent (Roberts et al. 2000b).

These examples indicate not only that banning DDT would increase mortality and morbidity due to malaria, but that the increases would occur relatively rapidly.

A recent study by Whitworth et al. (2000) raises the worrying possibility of interactions between HIV-1 and malaria. Their study showed that HIV-1 infection is associated with increased prevalence and intensity of *P. falciparum* infection in adults with acquired immunity to malaria, and that HIV-1 might also be associated with increased incidence of clinical malaria [see Taylor and Hoffman's (2000) commentary on the Whitworth study]. Given the prevalence of both HIV and malaria in Africa and that dealing with HIV is costlier and much more difficult, the Whitworth study reinforces the need for reducing exposure to malaria carriers.

Finally, DDT used for malaria control can also be effective in reducing other mosquito-borne diseases, such as leishmaniasis, dengue, and yellow fever (Davies et al. 1994, Severo 1955).

The Public Health Risks of *Not* Banning DDT

Some studies have suggested that contact with or ingestion of DDT could contribute to several ailments, including breast cancer, multiple myeloma, hepatic cancer, and non-Hodgkin's lymphoma. However, such effects have not been confirmed despite several efforts to replicate the studies (Attaran et al. 2000, A. G. Smith 2000). Smith (1991) notes, for instance, that there is no doubt that DDT causes tumors and changes in the liver in various types of rodents but not in some other animals, and that it is not clear how that relates to carcinoma in humans.

Other studies suggest that DDT may interfere with maternal lactation. It has also been suggested that DDT exposure in the uterus or in perinatal stages could have subtle effects on a child's development. Although those studies have been questioned, it is perhaps more significant for our purpose here that the public health effects are unclear (A. G. Smith 2000). The fact that the public health effects of DDT are disputed indicates that even if they are real, they are probably not of the same order of magnitude as either the 300 million malaria cases or the 1.1 million estimated deaths due to malaria in 1999—or they are delayed (WHO 1999a).

There are good reasons to question the relevance of historical epidemiological information regarding DDT's negative public health impacts. Notably, much of the DDT in aquatic and avian species that has found its way into human tissue is the result not of indoor DDT spraying but of past spraying for agricultural pest control. But because agricultural spraying has been largely discontinued worldwide and many countries who no longer have a major malaria problem have banned DDT, despite the absence of a global ban, DDT use dropped by 95 percent between 1981 and 1990 (Pesticide Action Network, undated).

Indoor spraying simply does not result in the same scale of environmental exposure as agricultural spraying. Attaran et al. (2000), for instance, estimate that Guyana's entire population at high risk of contracting malaria could be protected by the amount of DDT needed to spray 0.4 square kilometers of cotton. Indoor spraying has been estimated to have only 0.04 percent of the environmental impact as spraying an equivalent amount of DDT on agricultural fields (Attaran et al. 2000).

Because of the combination of reduced DDT use and lower environmental impacts from indoor spraying than from agricultural use, levels of DDT and its metabolites have been dropping in human and wildlife species for the past several decades. For instance, in the United States, amounts of DDT and related compounds found in national samples of freshwater fish declined 65 percent between 1971 and 1984 (Schmitt et al. 1990). Between 1980 and 1988, DDT in fall run coho salmon declined by 40 and 60 percent in Lakes Erie and Michigan, respectively (CEQ 1992). Between 1966 and 1985, levels of DDE (a derivative of DDT) in waterfowl dropped from 0.70 to 0.09 ppm in the Atlantic flyway, from 0.65 to 0.05 ppm in the Pacific flyway, and from 0.15 and 0.25 ppm to below detection levels in the Mississippi and Central flyways (CEQ 1993). And between 1974 and 1996, DDE levels in herring gull eggs from colonies in the five North American Great Lakes declined 85 to 93 percent (CEQ 1999).

Similarly, between the 1960s and 1990s, studies of various aquatic and avian species in the Baltic show that total DDT (including its metabolites) declined 8 to 12 percent per year for herring and cod and 11 percent per year in guillemot eggs (Olsson et al. 2000; Skei et al. 2000).

Perhaps most importantly, DDT in human adipose tissue dropped by 80 percent between 1970 and 1983 (USBOC 1987). In Canada, o,p'—and p,p'—DDT concentrations declined from 1.066 mg/kg of human adipose tissue to 0.066 milligrams per kilogram (UNEP/ GEMS 1991). DDT concentrations in human adipose tissue also dropped by an order of magnitude in the Netherlands.

Finally, based on a review of about 100 studies, Smith (1999) concludes that since 1975 DDT levels in human breast milk have declined 11 to 21 percent per year in the United States and Canada and between 9 and 13 percent per year in Western Europe. Notably, Smith's analysis suggests that DDT levels in human breast milk have also declined substantially since the early to mid-1970s in parts of

Asia, the Middle East, Latin America, and Eastern Europe, although data for those regions are more sparse.

All of these trends suggest that the public health benefits of a global ban on DDT would be even smaller than the putative impacts of past DDT use outlined above.

Applying the Precautionary Principle for Developing Countries

In order to establish whether or not the precautionary principle supports a particular course of action, it is necessary to use the framework presented previously to evaluate and weigh the risks that might be reduced—as well as those that might be generated—directly or indirectly by the implementation of that action.

We have already noted that malaria strikes 300 million people and kills over a million people each year, that indoor DDT spraying has proved to be a successful method of containing malaria, and that its effectiveness under real-world conditions (where costs and ease of use are critical) is often not matched by other theoretically available methods of malaria control. Thus, banning DDT would almost certainly increase the number of malaria cases and associated deaths beyond those that would otherwise occur. Based on historical experience, these effects would be manifested relatively soon after an effective ban was put in place. Even a small increase (say 5 percent) in the numbers would over a short period (say, 10 years) translate into 150 million additional cases and 550,000 deaths.

By contrast, the public health consequences of continuing or expanding indoor spraying of DDT are uncertain and, if they occur at all, would be delayed. Thus, in terms of reducing risks to public health, a global ban on DDT will almost certainly be counterproductive.

Applying the human mortality, uncertainty, and immediacy criteria to the public health impacts of banning DDT, one must conclude that the precautionary principle requires that indoor spraying of DDT be continued, and even encouraged, in developing countries where malaria continues to be a problem and where it can be reduced by such spraying, at least until equally cost-effective methods of controlling malaria are generally available.

If, and when, equally effective but cheaper options become available, become public knowledge, and are generally accepted as such by potential malaria victims and their public health officials, the marketplace will almost inevitably drive out DDT. (Why should anyone want to use an inferior product that is not cost-effective?) By the same token, if malaria-carrying mosquitoes were to become resistant to DDT to the extent that its use was no longer cost-effective in comparison with other options, economics once again would automatically phase out DDT use. Thus, it is superfluous to require that indoor spraying of DDT be phased out once cost-effective alternatives become available.

In fact, if the goal is to phase out DDT as soon as possible and without any counterproductive increases in human mortality, we should bolster programs to (a) research and develop safer and more cost-effective alternatives to DDT, (b) constantly monitor and evaluate the effectiveness and impacts of DDT and potential substitutes, and (c) disseminate such cost-effectiveness and impact-related information accurately to the general public and public health authorities in areas where malaria is or could become a problem.

It might be argued that for DDT the immediacy criterion may be invalid and overruled by the irreversibility criterion because, over time, DDT accumulation in the environment may lead to irreversible environmental harm. There are two counterarguments.

First, the death of a human being is as irreversible as, and more heinous than, the death, for instance, of a bird. That is, there is no moral equivalency between the two outcomes. Second, the experience of developed countries that have banned DDT indicates that its most critical adverse environmental effects—the declines in species such as the bald eagle, the peregrine falcon, and the osprey—are reversible, albeit slowly. Thus, in the United States, a quarter century after the ban on DDT, those avian species were no longer endangered (EDF 1997, Goklany 1998a). Such improvements are in accordance with the previously noted trends in DDT and its metabolites (e.g., DDE) in various fish and bird species, which are now a fraction of what they used to be (see, also, National Research Council 1999; Goklany 1994, 1996, 1998a). In other words, the experience of the developed world indicates that major environmental problems caused by DDT can eventually correct themselves.

It has also been argued that use of DDT should be discontinued because mosquitoes may develop resistance to it. But, as noted, the development of such resistance disables only one of the three pathways by which DDT acts to reduce malaria transmission. Moreover, as noted above, mosquitoes may also develop resistance to chemicals used to substitute for DDT—pyrethroids, for example. And if DDT is not used, what difference does it make whether mosquitoes develop any resistance? It makes more sense to use DDT until its use ceases to be cost-effective, for whatever reason (whether because of the buildup of resistance or the availability of more cost-effective alternatives). In fact, DDT's use buys time during which better alternatives can be developed and perfected while, in the meantime, reducing human mortality.

Because of the efficacy of DDT in containing malaria, it can be argued that it is critical that the development of DDT resistance among malaria carriers be slowed down as much as possible. Therefore, DDT uses other than indoor spraying should be discouraged where such spraying will contain malaria. Such a policy would be entirely consistent with the precautionary principle.

The improved health of the population resulting from reductions in malaria incidence will, in turn, have other indirect benefits for human well-being. First, a healthier population is more productive because it can devote more time and energy to economic pursuits (World Bank 1993, Barro 1997, WHO 1999a, Bloom 1999). Easterlin (1996), based on a United Nations study, notes that when malaria was eradicated in Mymensingh (now in Bangladesh), crop yields increased 15 percent because farmers could spend more time and energy on cultivation. In other areas, elimination of seasonal malaria enabled farmers to plant a second crop. According to the World Bank (1993, 18), the near-eradication of malaria in Sri Lanka between 1947 and 1977 is estimated to have raised that country's national income by 9 percent. A joint study by the Harvard University Center for International Development and the London School of Hygiene and Tropical Medicine concluded that if malaria had been eradicated in 1965, Africa's gross domestic product (GDP) would have been 32 percent higher today (*Guardian* 2000, HUCID and LSHTM 2000).

While healthier is wealthier, so is wealthier healthier (Pritchett and Summers 1996; Goklany 1999a, 2001a). Cross-country data show that infant mortality and life expectancy (surrogates for health as well as critical indicators of human well-being) improve as the level of economic development increases (see Figures 2-1 and 2-2; Goklany

FIGURE 2-1
INFANT MORTALITY VS. GDP PER CAPITA, 1997

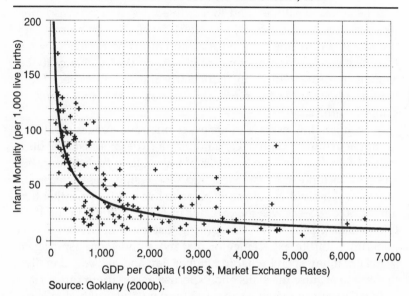

Source: Goklany (2000b).

FIGURE 2-2
LIFE EXPECTANCY VS. GDP PER CAPITA, 1997

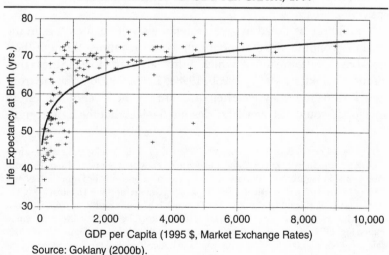

Source: Goklany (2000b).

23

2000b).[1] In fact, wealth and health reinforce each other in a virtuous cycle of progress (Goklany 1999a, 2001a).

A healthier, wealthier, and longer-lived population is also more likely to invest time, money, and effort developing its human capital, which in turn aids in the creation and diffusion of technology. In turn, that accelerates economic growth (Barro 1997, Goklany 2001a). Moreover, greater education, particularly of women, has been found to be an important factor in reducing mortality rates and improving public health.

In addition, the increase in life expectancy encourages greater investment in human capital (Goklany 2001a). The expected benefits to individuals, families, and societies of investing in higher education and postdoctoral research fellowships and residencies increase significantly if individuals are anticipated to live to 60 years rather than a mere 30 or so—as was the case, for instance, in India in the 1920s (Simon 2000). Thus, it is not surprising that levels of education have gone up with life expectancy or that more and more aspiring researchers today spend what in another day and age was literally a lifetime to acquire the skills and expertise necessary to pursue specialized careers in medicine, research, and institutes of higher learning. And those who have acquired these skills are then poised to help others follow the same path. Thus human capital breeds additional human capital, which further improves public health and strengthens economic growth.

In addition, as noted in greater detail elsewhere, increases in the level of economic development help countries move through their environmental transitions, which ultimately leads to a cleaner environment (Goklany 1995a, 1995b, 1998a, 1999a, 1999b). The environmental transition may well help account for the level of concern in developed countries over DDT despite the fact that the most signifi-

[1]Figures 2-1 and 2-2 are from Goklany (2000b). Economic development is measured as GDP per capita in 1995 U.S. dollars using market exchange rates (MXR). The continuous line in Figure 2-1 is fitted using a log-log relationship. For Figure 2-1, N and R^2 were 147 and 0.79, respectively. The slope of log (infant mortality) against log (GDP per capita) is significant ($p < 0.001$). For Figure 2-2, N = 148 and $R^2 = 0.65$. The continuous line is fitted using a log-linear relationship. The slope of life expectancy against log (GDP per capita) is also significant ($p < 0.001$). In both Figures, the x-axis scale is cut off at $7,000 to $10,000 per capita to better illustrate the dependence of infant mortality and life expectancy at low levels of economic development.

cant of their DDT-related environmental problems seem to be correcting themselves.

Finally, low fertility rates (i.e., low birth rates) are correlated with high levels of economic development, which also might help improve environmental quality (Goklany 1995a, 1998a, 1999a).

Applying the Precautionary Principle for Developed Countries

Although malaria was once prevalent in many of the richer countries, those countries have virtually no incidence of malaria today. DDT contributed significantly to the eradication of malaria in many advanced countries, including the United States (Zucker 1996, Bate 2000). However, today DDT plays virtually no role in reducing human mortality and improving public health in the developed countries. And if it did, those countries could afford equally safe and effective substitutes, despite any extra cost.

Therefore the major impact of DDT use in the richer countries would be its potential negative impacts on the environment and, more speculatively, on human health (NRC 1999). Thus, a ban on DDT in the richer countries—which most of them have, in fact, instituted—might be justified under a precautionary principle.

Applying the Precautionary Principle Worldwide

The above discussion indicates that prohibiting DDT use worldwide would most likely lead to substantial net increases in death and disease because the net harm caused by such a ban in the developing countries far outweighs its net benefits to the developed world. The harms are greater in magnitude and more certain and are likely to occur more rapidly than the benefits. Thus, under the precautionary principle, there ought not to be a global ban on DDT use.

However, we saw above that the precautionary principle prescribes vastly different policies when it is applied separately to developed countries and to developing countries where DDT use can reduce malaria's toll. Thus, a uniform global policy for DDT with identical requirements for all countries will be suboptimal, as are virtually all one-size-fits-all policies. If one insists on a uniform global policy, under a precautionary principle it must be one that encourages the indoor spraying of DDT.

Conclusion

The precautionary principle has been invoked to justify policies for a worldwide ban on DDT. However, these justifications are based on a selective application of the precautionary principle that considers the risks that might be reduced by such a ban but ignores the far larger, more certain, and more immediate risks that such a ban would inevitably bring in its wake. Specifically, these justifications overlook the likely outcome of a global DDT ban on human health and mortality in developing countries. Contrary to claims that a global ban on DDT use is based on caution, it would, in fact, increase the disease burden and overall risks to public health worldwide. In turn, economic development in malaria-endemic countries will continue to be adversely affected.

An evenhanded application of the precautionary principle—one that considers not only the public health and environmental risks that might be reduced by a global ban on DDT use but also the risks that might be generated in the real world—argues for a substantially different policy. Specifically, the precautionary principle argues that DDT use should not be banned worldwide because it will surely increase death and disease in human beings. In fact, indoor spraying of DDT ought to be encouraged in countries where such spraying would diminish malaria incidence. Such spraying should continue as long as equally safe and cost-effective substitutes are unavailable. It should be discontinued only after "informed consent" for a suspension of DDT spraying has been obtained from the beneficiaries of such spraying—that is, the populations at risk of contracting malaria.

In belated recognition of the public health benefits of DDT use in various developing countries, the World Wildlife Fund for Nature (WWF), for instance, dropped its call for a global DDT ban in 2007 (*Environmental Network News* 1998, WWF 2001). Such a ban would have been contrary to the precautionary approach.

If the ban had been promulgated, there would be only two possibilities in 2007. First, a cost-effective substitute is not found, in which instance the case for banning DDT use will be no stronger in 2007 than it is today. Second, a cost-effective substitute is indeed discovered, in which case economic considerations will prevail and use of DDT will be discontinued automatically. In either case there is little to be gained by writing a postponement into a legally binding international agreement. Instead of playing God with DDT and malaria by placing a deadline on global DDT use, it would be more fruitful to invest more heavily in research and development of alternative approaches to combat malaria more cost-effectively.

A better case can be made under the precautionary principle for a ban on DDT use in developed countries. Developed countries have rid themselves of malaria and, if the need should ever arise, they can afford substitutes. Thus access to DDT is no longer critical to protect their public health. Not surprisingly, many have already banned DDT use. As a result, environmental levels of DDT and its metabolites have dropped dramatically within their borders in the past quarter century. That has helped reduce and, in some cases, reverse DDT's environmental impacts, despite the absence of a global ban. So, although such a ban will do little harm to developed countries, it is far from clear that it will do much for public health or the environment.

In summary, a one-size-fits-all global ban on DDT use now or in the foreseeable future, despite its claim to be precautionary, would in fact be incautious because it is likely to add to the numbers of malaria deaths. Specifically, the precautionary principle supports a two-tiered approach toward DDT: that is, the policy for countries where malaria has been eradicated is different from that for countries where malaria is still prevalent or threatens to make a comeback.

In developed countries, a ban on DDT makes precautionary sense. On the other hand, in countries where malaria is an ongoing threat, indoor spraying of DDT ought to be encouraged until it is phased out automatically, if and when equally safe and cost-effective substitutes are available and have been accepted and adopted by the beneficiaries of indoor spraying in the developing world. Such an approach would avoid "silent springs" in the developed countries without silencing people in malaria-prone developing countries.

3. The Risks and Rewards of Genetically Modified Crops

Perhaps no human activity is more critical to human well-being and environmental quality than agriculture. Having sufficient food and adequate nutrition is the first step to better health; lower mortality rates; and a longer, more productive, and more fulfilling life (Goklany 1999a, 2001a).

At the same time, agriculture has literally shaped the world's landscape, rivers, and waterways. And its effects are often felt in estuaries, in oceans, and even in the atmosphere far from where the actual agricultural activities take place.

Agriculture is the human activity that has had the greatest effect on the world's biological diversity (Wilcove et al. 1998, Goklany 1998a). Today, agriculture alone accounts for 38 percent of global land area (FAO 2001), 66 percent of water withdrawals, and 85 percent of consumptive use worldwide (Shiklomanov 2000). It is also the major determinant of land clearance and habitat loss worldwide. Between 1980 and 1995, developing countries lost 190 million hectares of forest cover mainly because their increase in agricultural productivity was exceeded by growth in the demand for food; in the same period developed countries increased their forest cover by 20 million hectares because their productivity outpaced demand (FAO 1997). Agriculture and, to a lesser extent, forestry also affect biodiversity through water pollution and atmospheric transport—for example, by release of excess nutrients, pesticides, and silt into the environment (Wilcove et al. 1998, Goklany 1998a).

Demand for agricultural and forest products is almost certainly going to increase substantially. The world's population will almost inevitably grow from about 6 billion today to perhaps between 10 and 11 billion in 2100, an increase of 70 to 80 percent. The average person is likely to be richer, which ought to increase food demand per capita. It is probable that the predominant future environmental and natural resource challenge facing the globe will be the problem of meeting the human demand for food, nutrition, fiber, timber, and other natural resource products while conserving habitat and biodiversity (Goklany 1995a, 1998a, 1999a, 1999c, 2000a).

The question is whether biotechnology can help or hinder the reconciliation of these often opposing goals (Goklany 1995a, 1999c). Although most of the following discussion focuses on agriculture, with particular emphasis on developing countries, much of it is equally valid for other human activities that use land and water, such as forestry, and for developed countries as well.

Potential Environmental Benefits of Bioengineered Crops

According to 1998 UN projections, global population, which hit 6 billion in 1999, will most likely grow to 8.9 billion in 2050 (UNPD 1999). Figure 3-1, which is based on the methodology outlined in Goklany (1998a, 1999c), provides estimates of the additional land that would need to be converted to cropland from 1997 to 2050 as a function of the annual increase in productivity in the food and agricultural sector per unit of land. This figure assumes that global crop

FIGURE 3-1
NET HABITAT LOSS TO CROPLAND VS. INCREASE IN AGRICULTURAL
PRODUCTIVITY, 1997 TO 2050

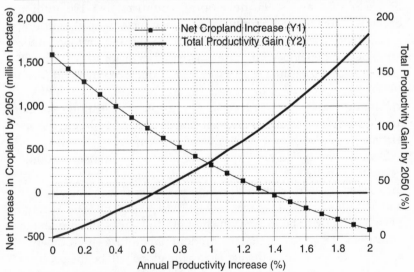

Source: FAO (2000) per Goklany (1998b, 2000a).

production per capita will grow at the same rate between 1997 and 2050 as it did between 1961 and 1963 and 1996 and 1998, and that new cropland will, on average, be as productive as existing cropland in 1997 (an optimistic assumption).

If the average productivity in 2050 is the same as it was in 1997—hardly a foregone conclusion (Goklany 1998a)—the entire increase in production (106 percent under the above assumptions of growth in population and food demand) will have to come from an expansion in global cropland. That would translate into additional habitat loss of at least 1,600 million hectares (see Figure 3-1) beyond the 1,510 million hectares devoted to cropland in 1997 (FAO 2000). Much of that expansion would necessarily come at the expense of forested areas (Goklany 1998a). It would lead to massive habitat loss and fragmentation, and put severe pressure on the world's remaining biodiversity and on *in situ* conservation.

On the other hand, a productivity increase of 1 percent per year, equivalent to a cumulative 69 percent increase from 1997 to 2050, would reduce the net amount of new cropland required to meet future demand to 325 million hectares. Such an increase in productivity is theoretically possible without resorting to biotechnology, provided sufficient investments are made in human capital and research and development, extension services, infrastructure expansion (to bring new land, where needed, into production and integrate it with the rest of the world's agricultural system), inputs such as fertilizers and pesticides, and the acquisition and operation of technologies to limit or mitigate environmental impacts of agriculture (Goklany 1998a, 1999c).

A 1 percent per year increase in the net productivity of the food and agricultural sector (per unit area) is within the bounds of historical experience: it increased 2 percent per year between 1961 and 1963 and 1996 and 1998 (FAO 2000). What is more important, there are many existing-but-underused opportunities to enhance productivity in an environmentally sound manner, but they are underused largely because of insufficient wealth—one reason why cereal yields are usually lower in poorer nations (Goklany 1998a, 1999c). Merely increasing the 1996–98 average cereal yields in developing and transition nations to the level attained by Belgium-Luxembourg (the country group that had the highest average yield) would have increased global production by 141 percent (calculated from FAO 2000); increasing the average global cereal yield [2.96 T/ha in

1996–98 (FAO 2000)] to that typical in Belgium-Luxembourg (7.80 T/ha in 1996–98) would increase global cereal production by 163 percent. Notably, the theoretical maximum yield is 13.4 T/ha or 350 percent greater than the average global cereal yield in 1996–98 (Linnemann et al. 1979).

Specifically, conventional (i.e., nonbioengineering) methods could be used to increase net productivity in the food and agricultural sector from farm to mouth by (a) further limiting preharvest crop losses to pests and diseases, which currently reduce global yields by an estimated 42 percent (Oerke et al. 1994); (b) increasing fertilizer use; (c) liming acidic soils; (d) adapting high-yield varieties to specific locations around the world, although many scientists believe that opportunities to further increase yields through conventional breeding techniques are almost tapped out (Conway and Toennissien 1999, Mann 1999a); and (e) reducing postharvest and end-use losses (Goklany and Sprague 1991), which are estimated at about 47 percent worldwide (Bender 1994). Moreover, precision farming could help reduce chemical and water use without reducing yields, which would reduce many of the adverse effects of modern agriculture.

Productivity improvements could be made much more rapidly and more surely with the aid of biotechnology. Biotechnology could more easily and quickly reduce current gaps between average yields and yield ceilings, and yield ceilings and the theoretical maximum yield, as well as push up the theoretical maximum yield. This begs the question as to whether such increases in productivity will also increase environmental costs and whether the productivity increases are sustainable in the long run. That issue will be discussed in greater detail later.

If the widespread adoption of biotechnology allowed agricultural productivity to increase from 1 percent to 1.5 percent per year, cropland could actually be *reduced* by 98 million hectares rather than increased by 325 million hectares (relative to 1997 levels), and at the same time the increased food demand of a larger and richer population could be met. That corresponds to a net increase in productivity of 30 percent in 2050 attributable to biotechnology alone. And if productivity is increased 2 percent per year, by 2050 at least 422 million hectares of cropland currently under plow could be returned to nature or made available for other human uses. That corresponds to a net improvement in productivity by 2050 of 69 percent due to biotechnology (Figure 3-1).

Several biotechnologically engineered crops, currently in various stages between research and commercialization, could increase yields and, more importantly, put more food on the table per unit of land and water diverted to agriculture. Such crops, which could be particularly useful in developing nations, include

- *Cereals that are tolerant of poor climatic and soil conditions*—specifically, cereals that can tolerate aluminum (they can grow in acidic soils), drought, high salinity levels, submergence, chilling, and freezing (De la Fuente et al. 1997, Apse et al. 1999, Kasuga et al. 1999, Swaminathan 1999, Conway and Toennissien 1999, Moffat 1999a, Zhang 1999, Pennisi 1998, Prakash 1998a; see also Jaglo-Ottosen et al. 1998). The ability to grow crops in such conditions could be critical for developing countries: 43 percent of tropical soils are acidic (World Bank 1994); more cropland is lost to high salinity than is gained through forest clearance; and salinity has rendered one-third of the world's irrigated land unsuitable for growing crops (Frommer et al. 1999). Moreover, if the world warms, the ability to tolerate drought, high salinity, submergence, and acidity could be especially important in achieving global food security. In Kasuga et al.'s (1999) experiments, 96.2 percent of genetically modified plants survived freezing compared with 9.5 percent of conventional plants. The corresponding numbers for drought were 76.7 percent vs. 1.8 percent and, for salinity stress, 78.6 percent vs. 17.9 percent.
- *Rice that combines the best traits of the African and Asian varieties*—the ability of African rice to shade out weeds when young and the high yield capacity of the Asian variety (Conway and Toennissien 1999). In addition, the GM variety is highly resistant to drought, pests, and diseases—a trait that could be particularly useful for Africa because its increases in rice yields have so far lagged behind those of the rest of the world. That lag is one reason why malnourishment in Sub-Saharan Africa has increased in the past several decades, in contrast to improved trends elsewhere (Goklany 1998a).
- *Rice that can close stomata more readily* (Mann 1999a). Use of such rice should increase the efficiency of water use and net photosynthetic efficiency. Both aspects will be useful under dry conditions—conditions that may become more prevalent in some areas as a result of global warming.

- *Rice with the alternative C4 pathway for photosynthesis.* This trait could be especially useful if there is significant warming because the C4 pathway is more efficient at higher temperatures (Ku et al. 1999, Edwards 1999, Conway and Toennissien 1999). In addition, efforts are under way to try to reengineer RuBisCO—an enzyme critical to all photosynthesis—by using RuBisCO from red algae, which is a far more efficient catalyst for photosynthesis than that found in crops (Mann 1999b).
- *Maize, rice, and sorghum that are resistant to* Striga, *a parasitic weed that could decimate yields in Sub-Saharan Africa* (Mann 1999c, MacIlwain 1999, Conway and Toennissien 1999).
- *Rice that has the ability to fix nitrogen* (IRRI 1999). Nitrogen, an essential plant nutrient, limits plant growth in much of the world. While ample supplies of nitrogen are available in the air and in the soil, little of it can be used directly by plants because it is not "fixed" in a form that plants can use directly. Hence the need for fertilizers containing "fixed" nitrogen. In the beginning of the 20th century, with resources of guano—a rich source of fixed nitrogen—running out, it seemed that global food production—and hence the world's population—was about to reach its limit. However, these fears were allayed with Fritz Haber's 1909 invention of a process to synthesize ammonia—a nitrogen fertilizer—from nitrogen in the air and hydrogen. For this signal achievement, which not only foreshadowed—but also made possible—the green revolution in the last third of the 20th century, Haber received the 1918 Nobel Prize for Chemistry. Nitrogen-fixing genetically modified crops would reduce humanity's dependence on synthetic nitrogen fertilizers, and the several environmental problems associated with their use, and overuse (see below). They would also reduce costs to farmers and consumers alike.
- *Rice and maize with enhanced uptake of phosphorus and nitrogen* (Conway and Toennissien 1999, Prakash 1998b, Inside Purdue 1998). Notably, these two crops account for 20 percent of global cropland.
- *Rice, maize, potato, sweet potato, and papaya that are resistant to insects, nematodes, bacteria, viruses, and fungi.* For instance, papaya, which had been ravaged in Hawaii by the papaya ringspot virus, has now made a comeback due to a bioengineered variety

resistant to that virus (Conway and Toennissien 1999, Ferber 1999).

- *Cassava, a staple in much of Africa, that is resistant to the cassava mosaic virus and including a gene with an enzyme (replicase) capable of disrupting the life cycles of a number of other viruses.* It is claimed that this GM cassava could increase yields 10-fold (Moffat 1999b). In addition, because cassava contains natural substances that can be converted to cyanide, it must be carefully prepared before consumption. Work is proceeding on producing a GM cassava that would be less toxic (Conway and Toennissien 1999).

- *Spoilage-prone fruits bioengineered for delayed ripening to increase their shelf life and reduce post-harvest losses.* Such fruits include bananas and plantains, important sources of food for many African nations (Conway and Toennissien 1999), and, in the United States, melons, strawberries, and raspberries (Lemaux 1999).

- *Crops bioengineered to reduce the likelihood of their seed pods shattering*—which reduces yields of crops such as wheat, rice, and canola. It is estimated that bioengineering could increase canola yields, for instance, by 25 percent to 100 percent (Liljegren et al. 2000).

- *High-lysine maize and soybeans, maize with high oil and energy content, and forage crops with lower lignin content*—which ought to improve livestock feed and reduce the overall demand for land needed for livestock (Mazur et al. 1999, Conway and Toennissien 1999).

If the methods and genes used to bioengineer those crops can be successfully adapted and transferred to other vegetables, tubers, fruits, and even trees, it would help reduce the amount of land and water needed in the future to feed, clothe, and shelter human populations, and it would free up those resources for the rest of nature.

Use of the GM crops described above, by increasing crop yields and reducing the amount of cultivated land, would also reduce the area subject to soil erosion from agricultural practices. That, in turn, would limit associated environmental effects on water bodies and aquatic species and reduce the loss of carbon sinks and stores into the atmosphere. Furthermore, many of the same GM crops could also directly reduce nutrients and pesticides released into the environment (Goklany 2000d, 2001b). These bioengineered crops include

- *Nitrogen-fixing rice and rice and maize bioengineered with the ability to increase uptake of phosphorus and nitrogen from the soil.* In Europe and the United States, only 18 percent of the nitrogen and 30 percent of the phosphorus in fertilizers are incorporated into crops, between 10 and 80 percent of the nitrogen and 15 percent of the phosphorus end up in aquatic ecosystems, and much of the remainder accumulates in the soil, to be later eroded into aquatic systems (Carpenter et al. 1998). Nitrogen-fixing crops would reduce reliance on fertilizers and thereby reduce ground and surface water pollution, risks of chemical spills, and atmospheric emissions of nitrous oxide (N_2O), a greenhouse gas that, pound for pound over a 100-year period, is 310 times more potent a greenhouse gas than CO_2 (IPCC 1996b).

- *Crops resistant to viruses, weeds, and other pests*—for example, *Striga*-resistant maize, rice, and sorghum. Examples also include various *Bt* crops containing genes from the *Bacillus thuringiensis* bacterium, which has been used in insecticide spray for four decades. Carpenter and Gianessi (2001: 4) estimate that in 1999 the planting of *Bt* cotton on 32 percent of U.S. cotton areage reduced chemical pesticide use by over 2.7 million pounds, increased yields by 260 million pounds, and netted farmers $99 million. Although the use of *Bt* corn—which is planted on 26 percent of the acreage used to grow corn in the United States—resulted in a drop in farmers' revenues of $35 million, pesticide use dropped by 1 million acre-treatments, and production increased by 66 million bushels, equivalent to the output of half a million acres (Carpenter and Gianessi 2001: 4). Developing countries also can reduce the use of pesticides by using pest-resistant crops. For example, in India—the world's third largest producer of cotton—cotton occupies only 5 percent of the land yet cotton farmers buy about 50 percent of all pesticides used in the country (Prakash 1999). In 1998, the devastation caused by pests reportedly contributed to 500 suicides among Indian cotton farmers whose crops had failed. Field trials of *Bt* cotton at 30 locations in India show a 14 to 38 percent increase in yield despite suspension of all spraying (Hindu Business Line 2000).

- *Low-phytic-acid corn and soybean and phytase feed*—which help livestock better digest and absorb phosphorus. This would reduce phosphorus in animal waste and decrease runoff into streams, lakes, and other water bodies, mitigating one of the major sources of excess nutrients in the environment (Grabau Laboratory 1998, Mikesell 1999, CeresNet 1999). It would also reduce the need for inorganic phosphorus supplements in feed.

- *Crops tolerant of various herbicides*—so that those herbicides can be used to kill weeds but not the crop itself. Herbicide-tolerant crops are among the most common applications of biotechnology today. One commercially available example is "Roundup Ready" soybean, which is engineered to be tolerant to glyphosate. Such crops could help reduce the amount, toxicity, and/or persistence of pesticides. Planting of such crops seems to have reduced application of more hazardous and longer-lasting herbicides (e.g., acetochlor), although overall herbicide use may have increased (Ferber 1999). Gianessi and Carpenter (2001: 3–4) estimate that U.S. farmers who planted Roundup Ready soybean (which was planted on 47 percent of soybean acreage) lowered weed control costs by $216 million (equivalent to 19 million acre-treatments). Second, such crops would also increase yields while facilitating no-till cultivation, which, by stemming soil erosion, protects future agricultural productivity. Moreover, erosion can be particularly damaging to the environment because the eroded particles can transport fertilizers and pesticides into aquatic systems and into the atmosphere. Finally, as noted, soil erosion releases stored carbon into the atmosphere.

Bioengineered crops can also be engineered to directly clean up environmental problems. For instance, GM plants can be developed that selectively absorb various metals and metal complexes such as aluminum, copper, and cadmium from contaminated soils (Moffat 1999b). Such plants could, for example, detoxify methyl mercury in soils, removing it from the food chain.

Researchers have also genetically modified aspen trees to produce 50 percent less lignin and 15 percent more cellulose. Lignin, a component of all wood, must be chemically separated from cellulose to make the pulp used in paper production. The GM tree has half the normal lignin-to-cellulose ratio of about 1:2. Overall, 15 percent more pulp may be produced from the same amount of wood. Moreover, the GM trees are 25–30 percent taller. Thus, the amount of land, chemicals, and energy required to make a given quantity of paper should to be reduced substantially, as should the environmental impacts at every stage, from tree farming to paper production (MTU 1999).

Other potential applications of biotechnology that could reduce environmental impacts include production of biodegradable plastics using oilseed rape and colored cotton (which could reduce reliance on synthetic dyes) (Lawrence 1999).

Public Health Benefits of Bioengineered Crops

Having sufficient quantities of food is often the first step to a healthy society (WHO 1999a, Goklany 1999a). The increase in food supplies per capita during the past half-century is a major reason for the worldwide improvement in human health during that period. Between 1961 and 1997, food supplies per capita increased 23 percent (FAO 1999a). Thus, despite a 40 percent increase in population between 1969–71 and 1994–96, chronic undernourishment in developing countries dropped from 35 percent to 19 percent of their population (FAO 1999b), which in turn helped lower global infant mortality rates from 156 to 57 per 1,000 live births (between 1950–55 and 1998), increase life expectancies from 46.5 to 65.7 years (between 1950–55 and 1997), and enable the average person to live a more fulfilling and productive life (WHO 1999a; UNDP 1999; Goklany 1999a, 2001a).

Despite unprecedented progress during the 20th century, billions of people still suffer from undernourishment, malnutrition, and other ailments attributable, in whole or in part, to insufficient food or poor nutrition. Table 3-1 lists the current extent and consequences of some of these food- and nutrition-related problems, and a qualitative assessment of the likelihood that using GM rather than conventional crops could reduce their extent or severity.

Table 3-1 shows that about 825 million people around the world are currently undernourished (i.e., cannot meet their basic needs for energy and protein) (FAO 1999b). Reducing those numbers over the next half-century—while also reducing pressures on biodiversity despite anticipated population increases of 1.3 to 4.7 billion (UNPD 1999)—requires increasing the quantity of food produced per unit of

Table 3-1
Public health problems related to insufficient food or poor nutrition, and the likelihood that they could be alleviated using GM crops

Problem	Current Extent (Year)	Likelihood That GM Crops Would Reduce Problem
Undernourishment	825 million people (1994–96)	Very high
Malnutrition	6.6 million deaths per year in children < 5 years of age (1995)	Very high
Stunting	200 million people (1995)	High
Iron-deficiency anemia	2,000 million people (1995)	High
Vitamin A deficiency	260 million people (1995)	High
Ischemic and cerebrovascular diseases	2.8 million deaths per year in HIC (1998); 9.7 million deaths per year in LIC/MIC (1998) (includes those caused by smoking)	Moderate
Cancers	2.0 million deaths per year in HIC (1998); 5.2 million deaths per year in LIC/MIC (1998) (includes those caused by smoking)	Moderate

Source: WHO 1999a, 1999b, 1999c; FAO 1999b.
NOTE: HIC = high-income countries; LIC = low-income countries; MIC = middle-income countries.

land and water. As discussed above, GM crops could help in that struggle.

But increasing the quantity of food is not enough. Improving the nutritional quality of food is just as important. The diets of over half the world's population are deficient in iron, vitamin A, and other micronutrients (see Table 3-1). Such deficiencies can cause disease, if not death (WHO 1999a, FAO 1999b). About 2 billion people do not have enough iron in their diet and are thus susceptible to anemia. Another 260 million suffer from vitamin A deficiency, which causes clinical xerophthalmia, a condition that if untreated, may lead to blindness, especially in children. Vitamin A is also crucial for effective functioning of the immune system (WHO 1999b). Through the cumulative effect of these deficiencies, malnutrition in 1995 was responsible for 6.6 million or 54 percent of deaths worldwide in children under five, stunted growth in another 200 million children, and clinical xerophthalmia in about 2.7 million people (WHO 1999c).

In addition to ensuring that adequate quantities of food are available, bioengineering could also help reduce many of those micronutrient deficiencies. For instance, Swiss scientists have developed "golden rice"—rich in betacarotene, a precursor to vitamin A—and crossed it with another bioengineered strain rich in iron and in cysteine, which allows iron to be absorbed in the digestive tract. Such rice would help reduce vitamin A and iron deficiency–related deaths and diseases in the developing world. Iron-fortified rice, whether golden or not, would also reduce the need for meat, one of the primary sources of dietary iron. As a result, overall demand for livestock feed—and the land, water, and other factors needed to produce that feed—might be reduced (Gura 1999, Guerinot 2000, Ye et al. 2000; see also Goto et al. 1999).

Scientists are also working on using bananas and other fruits as vehicles to deliver vaccines against the Norwalk virus, E. coli, hepatitis B, and cholera (Moffat 1999b, Smaglik 1998), eventually leading to low-cost, efficient immunization of whole populations against common diseases, with broader coverage than is likely with conventional needle immunization.

Bioengineered crops can also help battle the so-called "diseases of affluence": ischemic heart disease, hypertension, and cancer. In 1998, according to the World Health Organization (1999a), those diseases accounted for 4.8 million or 60 percent of the total deaths in high-income countries and 14.9 million or 32 percent of deaths in low- and middle-income countries (Table 3-1). There are several GM crops that can help reduce this toll. For instance, genetically enhanced soybeans that are lower in saturated fats are already on the market. The International Food Information Council (1999) notes that biotechnology could also make soybean, canola, and other oils and their products, such as margarine and shortenings, more healthful. Bioengineering could also produce peanuts with improved protein balance; tomatoes with increased antioxidant content; potatoes with higher starch than conventional potatoes, which ought to reduce the amount of oil absorbed during the processing of foods like French fries or potato chips; fruits and vegetables fortified with or containing higher levels of vitamins such as C and E; and higher-protein rice, containing genes transferred from pea plants.

Moreover, levels of mycotoxins, which apparently increase with insect damage in crops, are lower in *Bt* corn. Some mycotoxins, such as fumonisin, can be fatal to horses and pigs and may be human carcinogens (Munkvold and Hellmich 1999). Morton (2001) argues that GM *Bt* food crops are safer than conventional crops sprayed with *Bt* because the sprays contain several toxins that could affect both insects and mammals, whereas the GM variety contains a single toxin known to be harmful to insects but not to mammals. Thus, *Bt* corn, whether used as food for humans or feed for livestock, may be safer and healthier than conventional corn.

GM plants may be further able to save life and limb if they can be successfully engineered to biodegrade explosives around land mine and abandoned munitions sites (Bolin 1999, French et al. 1999).

Finally, to the extent that pest-resistant GM plants can reduce the amount, toxicity, and persistence of pesticides used in agriculture (by themselves or as parts of integrated pest management systems), it would reduce accidental poisonings and other harmful health effects on farm workers. For instance, there have apparently have been instances of food poisoning and human infections from *Bt* sprays but none (so far) from *Bt* crops (Morton 2001).

Adverse Environmental Consequences from Bioengineered Crops

The major environmental concerns regarding GM crops are those related to crops that are designed to be resistant to pests or tolerant of herbicides. One potential risk is that target pests will become resistant to toxins produced by pest—resistant GM crops, such as *Bt* corn or *Bt* cotton. Although that is a possibility even if *Bt* is delivered via conventional sprays on non-GM plants, it is argued that it is of greater concern with *Bt* plants because with conventional spraying target pests are exposed to *Bt* toxins for only brief periods, whereas currently available *Bt* crops produce toxins throughout the growing season, which could increase the chances of developing *Bt*-resistant pests (Gould 1998; see also Walliman 2000). Moreover, some laboratory studies suggest that target pests may develop resistance more rapidly than had previously been thought possible (Liu et al. 1999, Agbiotechnet 1999). However, subsequent studies from Arizona, Mississippi, and Australia indicate that contrary to these prognostications, bollworm, for instance, did not increase its resistance to *Bt* toxin produced by a GM *Bt* cotton (Tabashnik et al. 2000, Kershen 2001).

It has also been argued that the only known insect resistance to *Bt* is caused by *Bt* sprays (Morton 2001). This has been attributed to the adaptation of conventional strategies (developed to deter pest resistance due to conventional pesticide) to GM crops. Such strategies include ensuring that plants deliver high doses of *Bt* while simultaneously maintaining refuges for non-*Bt* crops so that pest populations remain susceptible to *Bt*. In fact, the Environmental Protection Agency has established the requirement that *Bt* corn farmers plant 20 percent of their land in non-*Bt* corn, as refuges. For *Bt* corn grown in cotton areas, farmers must plant at least 50 percent non- *Bt* corn (EPA 2000a). EPA also requires expanded monitoring to detect any potential resistance. Other strategies to delay development of pesticide resistance include crop rotation (Gould 1998); developing crops with more than one toxin gene acting on separate molecular targets (Conway 2000); and inserting the bioengineered gene into the chloroplast, which ought to express *Bt* toxin at higher levels (Daniell 1999, Kota et al. 1999). Notably, farmers have an economic stake in implementing such adaptive strategies so that their crop losses to pests are kept in check in the long, and the short, term.

Another source of risk is that *Bt* from pest-resistant plants could harm, if not kill, nontarget species. That could happen if, for instance, *Bt*-laden pollen were to drift away from the field or if the toxin were to leak through the roots and be consumed by nontarget organisms susceptible to the *Bt* toxin (Losey et al. 1999, Walliman 2000, Saxena et al. 1999). However, a recent study suggests that such root leakage is quite unlikely to either kill non-target pests or, for that matter, cause *Bt* to accumulate in non-*Bt* crops grown subsequently on the same soil (Saxena and Stotzky 2001). But in a laboratory study that captured headlines around the world, and stoked the flames of the anti-GM cause, Losey et al. (1999) indicated a 44 percent mortality rate for monarch butterfly larvae fed on milkweed dusted with *Bt* corn pollen compared with zero for the control case (which used milkweed dusted with ordinary pollen). In a more sophisticated study, Jesse and Obrycki (2000) found a 20 percent mortality rate for monarch butterfly larvae fed in the laboratory with leaves exposed to pollen in or near a field of *Bt* plants.

However, whether—and the extent to which—the monarch butterfly population would be affected in the real world is a matter of debate (Ferber 1999, Richard 2000). One study suggests that under a worst-case scenario as much as 7 percent of the North American population (estimated at 100 million) may die, although the real-world effect would probably be smaller (Ferber 1999; see also Milius 1999). Some have also argued that the major threat to monarchs is the habitat loss in their wintering grounds in Mexico (Lewis and Palevitz 1999; see also Sheridan 2000), which is a result of pressure from a growing population in need of land.

Notably, in a recent analysis, EPA (2000b) concluded that based on their examination, "the weight of evidence" indicates "no hazard to wildlife from the continued registration of *Bt* crops." The Agency also concluded that continued cultivation of *Bt* corn is unlikely to "cause harmful widespread effects to monarch butterflies at this time." It also noted that the only endangered species of concern are in the lepidoptera and coleoptera group (i.e., butterflies, moths, and beetles), but the majority of those species have very restricted habitat range and do not feed in, or close to the *Bt* crop planting areas. Perhaps more importantly, the inadvertent effects of *Bt* crops due to pollen dispersal or root leakage could be virtually eliminated by bioengineering genes into the chloroplast rather than into nuclear DNA (Kota et al. 1999, Scott and Wilkinson 1999, Chamberlain and Stewart 1999).

Bt could also enter the food chain through root leakage or if predators prey on target pests. For instance, studies have shown that green lacewing larvae, a beneficial insect, that ate maize borers fed with *Bt* maize were more likely to die (Hilbeck et al. 1998). But the real-world significance of this has also been disputed based on the long history of *Bt* spraying on crops and other studies that have shown beneficial insects essentially unharmed by such spraying, particularly under field conditions (Gray 1998; Wraight et al. 2000).

There is also a concern that bioengineered genes from herbicide- or pest-tolerant crops might escape into wild relatives, leading to "genetic pollution" and creating "superweeds." That would have an adverse economic impact on farmers, reducing crop yields and detracting from the very justification for using such GM crops (Gray and Raybould 1998). Clearly, the farmer has a substantial incentive for preventing weeds from acquiring herbicide tolerance and, if that fails, to keep such weeds in check.

Gene escape is possible if sexually compatible wild relatives are found near fields planted with GM crops, as is the case in the United States for sorghum, oats, rice, canola, sugar beets, carrots, alfalfa, sunflowers, and radishes (Mann 1999c, Regal 1994, Lemaux 1999). However, the most common GM crops—soybeans and corn—have no wild U.S. relatives (Cook 1999, Mann 1999c). As the Royal Society (1998) pointed out in its assessment of the issue, centuries of conventional breeding have rendered a number of important crops, such as, maize and wheat, "ecologically incompetent" in many areas. It also noted that despite the use of conventionally bred herbicide-tolerant plants, there has been no upsurge in problems related to herbicide-tolerant weeds (Royal Society 1998). Although these theoretical arguments by themselves do not guarantee safety (Regal 1994), they seem confirmed by Crawley et al.'s (2001) 10-year-long British study of four different herbicide-tolerant or pest-resistant GM crops (oilseed rape, corn, sugar beet, and potato) and their conventional counterparts grown in 12 different habitats. That study indicated that within four years all plots of rape, corn, and beet had died out naturally. Only one plot of potatoes survived the 10th year, but that was a non-GM variety. In other words, GM plants were no more invasive or persistent in the wild than their conventional counterparts. And had any herbicide-tolerant or pest-resistant weeds begun to spread, available crop management techniques (such as another herbicide) could have been used to control them.

The Crawley et al. study also provides reassurance with respect to another potential environmental concern: that herbicide-tolerant or pest-resistant "superweeds" could invade natural ecosystems. The study confirms that such GM plants do not have a competitive advantage in a natural system unless that system is treated with the herbicide in question. But if it were so treated, would it still qualify as a natural system? Moreover, if it had to be treated, another herbicide to which the so-called superweed is not resistant could be used. On the other hand, if the area is not treated with the herbicide in question, what difference does it make to the ecosystem whether the weed is tolerant? And what is the significance of "genetic pollution" with respect to ecosystem function and biodiversity? Would gene escape affect ecosystem function negatively? Does gene escape diminish or expand biodiversity?

To bring this issue into focus, consider the case of human beings. If an Indian from Calcutta came to Washington, D.C., and had an offspring with a native-born American, would that not, as the term has been used, be considered "genetic pollution"? (Not very long ago, xenophobes labeled that miscegenation.) Does that diminish or expand biological diversity? Is such genetic pollution acceptable for human beings but not for other species? But if the answer varies with the species, it raises questions about the validity of the notion that gene escape can be equated to pollution—genetic or otherwise (Goklany 2000c; see also Sagoff 1999, Rayl 1999, and, for a different viewpoint, Johnson 1999).

In addition, genes may escape from GM crops to non-GM crops of the same species. If that were to occur, it would be unpopular with organic farmers, who are afraid it might "adulterate" their produce, and with producers and farmers of GM seeds, who are not eager to have someone else profit from their investments. Crawley et al.'s study is consistent with the Royal Society's (1998) prognosis that because more crops (including corn, sorghum, sugar beets, and sunflowers) are now grown from hybrid seeds, that provides a measure of built-in security against such gene transfers. Moreover, the chances of such gene escape can be further reduced by maintaining a buffer between the two crops.

Of course, gene escape could be limited with greater certainty if the GM plant were engineered to be sterile or were prevented from germinating by using, for instance, "terminator technology." An alternative approach would be to insert the gene into the chloroplast, which would preclude spread through pollen or fruit and prevent root leakage (Daniell 1999, Royal Society 1998).

Finally, there is a concern that in the quest to expand yields GM plants will work too well in eliminating pests and weeds, and that this will lead to a further simplification of agricultural ecosystems and a further decrease in biodiversity. That concern, in conjunction with the other noted environmental concerns, needs to be weighed against the cumulative biodiversity and other environmental benefits of reduced conversion of habitat to cropland, and decreased use of chemical inputs.

Adverse Public Health Consequences of Bioengineered Crops

A major health concern is that the new genes inserted into GM plants could be incorporated into a consumer's genetic makeup. However, there is no evidence that any genes have ever been transferred to human beings through food or drink despite the fact that plant and animal DNA has always been a part of the daily human diet (Royal Society 1998). In fact, an estimated 4 percent of the human diet is composed of DNA (Chassy and Sheppard 1999), and an average adult Briton consumes 150,000 km of DNA in an average meal (Lewis and Palevitz 1999). Moreover, it is unclear whether consuming, for instance, beans that have been genetically modified with genes from a pig would pose a greater risk to public health than consuming a dish of non-GM pork-and-beans.

Another concern is that genes transferred from foods to which many people are allergic could trigger allergies in unsuspecting consumers of such GM crops. Between 1 and 3 percent of the adults and between 5 and 8 percent of the children in the United States suffer from food allergies. Each year food allergies cause 135 fatalities and 2,500 emergency room visits (Buchanan 1999).

The concern regarding allergic reactions to GM foods can be traced to precommercialization tests conducted by Pioneer Hi-Bred, which showed that a soybean that had been bioengineered to boost its nutritional quality by using a gene from the Brazil nut was, in fact, allergenic. Although this example shows that GM foods can be tested prior to commercialization for their allergic potential, opponents of GM foods have used this as an argument against bioengineered crops. Several databases of known allergens could be used to help identify problematic GM products before they are developed (Royal Society 1998, Gendel 1999). In fact, because bioengineering allows more precise manipulation of genes than does conventional plant breeding, it could be used to render allergenic crops nonallergenic (Buchanan 1999, Scalise 1997).

Yet another potential negative effect on public health is that antibiotic resistant "marker" genes, which are used to identify whether a gene has been successfully incorporated into a plant, could, through consumption of the antibiotic gene by humans, accelerate the trend toward antibiotic-resistant diseases. However, by comparison with the threat posed by the use of antibiotics in feed for livestock and their overuse as human medicines, the increased risk due to such markers is slight (Royal Society 1998; see also FAO/WHO 1996, May 1999, Ferber 2000, *Science* 2000).

Applying the Precautionary Principle

The above discussion indicates that there are risks associated with both the use and the nonuse of GM crops. Here I will apply the criteria outlined in the framework presented in Chapter 1 for evaluating actions that could result in uncertain costs and benefits. Ideally, each criterion should be applied, one at a time, to the consequences of GM crop use (or nonuse) for human mortality, public health, and the environment. However, because there are variations in the severities, certainties, and magnitudes associated with the various competing costs and benefits of each of these sets of consequences, one may have to apply several criteria simultaneously.

Public Health Consequences

Population could increase 50 percent between 1998 and 2050 (from 5.9 billion to 8.9 billion, according to the best UN estimate). Hence, by 2050, one ought to expect that undernourishment, malnutrition, and their consequences—death and disease—would also increase by 50 percent worldwide, if the global food supply increases by a like amount and all else remains equal. Thus, according to Table 3-1, which provides estimates for the prevalence of such problems in the mid- to late-1990s, unless food production outstrips population growth significantly over the next half century, billions in the developing world may suffer annually from undernourishment, hundreds of millions from stunted growth, and millions may die from malnutrition.

Based on the sheer magnitude of people at risk of hunger and malnutrition, and the degree of certainty regarding the public health consequences, one can state with confidence that limiting GM crops will, by limiting the rate at which food production can expand, almost certainly increase death and disease, particularly among the world's poor.

GM crops could also reduce or postpone deaths due to diseases of affluence. Although the probability that that might occur is lower than the probability of reducing deaths from hunger and malnutrition, the expected number of deaths postponed could run into the millions. A 10 percent decrease, for instance, in today's 15 million annual deaths from cancer and ischemic and cerebrovascular diseases translates into 1.5 million lives saved each year (see Table 3-1). And those numbers could increase in the future as populations increase and become older.

By contrast, the negative public health consequences of ingesting GM foods are speculative (e.g., the effects due to ingesting transgenes), relatively minor in magnitude (e.g., a potential increase in antibiotic resistance), or both (e.g., increased incidence of allergic reactions). Moreover, it is possible to contain, if not eliminate, the effects of even those impacts. As noted previously, the likelihood of allergic reactions can be reduced by checking various databases of known allergens prior to developing a GM crop and by testing food from such crops prior to commercialization. Progress is also being made with respect to the risk of increasing antibiotic resistance. Novartis has developed a sugar-based alternative to antibiotic-resistant marker genes that has been used to develop about a dozen GM crops, including maize, wheat, rice, sugar beets, oilseed rape, cotton, and sunflowers (Coghlan 1999). With additional research, it ought to be possible to devise alternative marker genes for other crops or develop practical methods to remove or repress antibiotic-resistant marker genes (Royal Society 1998, Harding 1999).

Thus, based on the *uncertainty*, *expectation value*, and *adaptation criteria* applied either singly or in conjunction, use of genetic modification must be favored over nonuse. Hence, the precautionary principle *requires* that we continue to research, develop, and commercialize (with appropriate safeguards, of course) those GM crops that would increase food production and generally improve nutrition and health, especially in the developing world.

Some have argued that many developed countries are "awash in surplus food" (see, e.g., Williams 1998) and have no need to boost food production. However, that argument ignores the fact that reducing those surpluses would be almost as harmful to public health in developing countries as curtailing those countries' own food production. At present, net cereal imports of the developing countries exceed 10 percent of their production (FAO 2001). Without trade (and aid) that moves the surplus production in developed countries voluntarily to developing countries suffering from food deficits, food supplies in developing countries would be lower, food prices would be steeper, undernourishment and malnutrition would be higher, and associated health problems, such as illness and premature mortality, would be greater. As already noted, developing countries' food deficits are expected to increase in the future because of high population growth rates and possibly further worsened by global warming. Therefore, the food surpluses of developed countries will be at least as critical for future food security in developing countries as they are today (Goklany 1998a, 1999c).

The preceding argument against GM crops implicitly assumes that such crops will provide little or no public health benefits to the inhabitants of developed countries (net environmental benefits are addressed below). As noted above, GM crops are also being engineered to improve nutrition in order to combat diseases of affluence afflicting populations in developed, as well as developing, nations. Such diseases, which are major causes of premature death worldwide, kill about 4.8 million annually in the developed countries (WHO 1999a, Table 3-1).

If the use of GM crops were to produce even a small reduction in these numbers it would translate into relatively large declines in the death tolls of developed countries. The health benefits of "golden rice," for instance, do not have to be confined to developing countries; developed countries, too, could avail themselves of its benefits. Thus even for developed countries, the magnitude and certainty of the potential public health benefits of GM crops far outweigh the speculative health consequences of ingesting GM foods.

Another argument against using GM foods to increase food production is that, because there is no shortage of food in the world today and the problem of hunger and malnutrition is rooted in poor distribution and unequal access to food because of poverty, it is unnecessary to increase food production; therefore, there is no compelling need for biotechnology (MacIlwain 1999). Significantly, that argument tacitly acknowledges that GM crops would boost production (and productivity). The rest of the argument, however, is flawed.

First, while unequal access is a perennial problem—one that continues to persist despite the successes of conventional agriculture—

the argument misses the point. The case for bioengineered crops is not that it is the one and only solution for solving hunger and malnutrition. Increasing food production and improving access are not mutually exclusive. It should be sufficient that GM crops can contribute to the solution and that they are among the most efficient solutions for the problem.

Conventional agriculture has been relatively successful in improving global access to food. The evidence lies in the fact that hunger and malnourishment have declined substantially in the past few decades despite a substantial increase in population. The principal reasons for these improvements are production increases that outstripped population growth and brought food prices down worldwide; economic growth, which made food more affordable to all, particularly in developing countries; investments in infrastructure, which enable rapid and efficient distribution of agricultural products; and greater democratization, which increases the political accountability of rulers to those ruled (Goklany 1998a, 1999c).

Although GM crops (in comparison with conventional crops) are unlikely to directly increase democratization or economic growth, they can indirectly boost the latter. Moreover, as the anti-GM crop argument (that there is sufficient food) seems to recognize, GM crops could increase productivity more rapidly and by larger amounts, which would further increase food availability and reduce costs to consumers. In addition, one of the problems contributing to poor distribution is spoilage of crops before they are consumed. As noted, various GM crops could increase shelf life and reduce spoilage and wastage. GM crops cannot guarantee equal access, but they can improve access for the poorer segments of society more rapidly than can conventional crops.

Second, if the argument that there is sufficient food is truly a compelling one against GM crops, it should be equally valid for increases in production using conventional technologies. If that is indeed the case, perhaps developing countries like India and Bangladesh should forego increasing agricultural productivity altogether and focus only on improving access and distribution. For obvious reasons, no one makes this argument.

Third, this argument completely overlooks the fact that GM crops can improve the nutritional quality, and not merely the quantity of food, which as Table 3-1 shows can contribute substantially to reductions in human mortality and morbidity.

Environmental Consequences

A figure similar to Figure 3-1 could be developed for any level of food demand, whether it is, say, half that of today (perhaps because of a perfect cost- or transaction-free distribution system and a magical equalization of income) or whether it is four times that (possibly due to runaway population growth). Regardless of the level of demand, limiting GM crops would lower crop and forest yields per unit of land and water used. As Figure 3-1 shows, to compensate for the lower yields, more land and water would have to be pressed into mankind's service, leaving that much less for the rest of nature (Goklany 1998a, 1999c).

Reductions in the amount of land and water available for the rest of nature would be further aggravated by the fact that the price of land and water, relative to other goods, would rise, as would the opportunity costs for those resources (Goklany 1998a). As a result, the socioeconomic costs of setting aside land or water for conservation and preservation of nature would increase, further inhibiting *in situ* conservation of species and biodiversity, which is one of the major goals of the Convention on Biological Diversity, beyond the goal of merely conserving biodiversity itself (Glowka et al. 1994: 11) (see the discussion of those goals in the next section).

If bioengineering succeeds in improving the protein and micronutrient content of vegetables, fruits, and grains, it might persuade many more people to adopt and, more importantly, persevere with vegetarian diets, thereby reducing the additional demand meat-eating places on land and water. In addition, giving up GM crops will, more likely than not, further increase the pressures on biodiversity caused by excess nutrients, pesticides, and soil erosion. Finally, reduced conversion of habitat and forest to cropland and timberland, coupled with reductions in soil erosion due to increased no-till cultivation, would further limit deterioration of water quality and losses of carbon reservoirs and sinks.

Arrayed against these benefits to ecosystems, biodiversity, and carbon stores and sinks are the environmental costs of limiting pest-resistant and herbicide-tolerant GM crops *minus* the environmental costs of conventional farming practices. These costs include a potential increase in the diversity of the flora and fauna associated with or in the immediate vicinity of GM crops if they are more effective in reducing nontarget pests and weeds than conventional farming prac-

51

tices, and the possible consequences of gene escape to weeds and non-GM crops.

Therefore, with respect to the environmental consequences of the use or nonuse of GM crops, one must conclude, based on the *uncertainty* and *expectation value criteria*, that the precautionary principle requires the cultivation of GM crops. On balance, GM crops should conserve the planet's habitat, biodiversity, and carbon stores and sinks, provided due caution is exercised, particularly with respect to herbicide-tolerant and pest-resistant GM crops.

It may be argued that although gene escape to "natural" ecosystems might be a low-probability event, it may cause irreversible harm to the environment; thus, under the *irreversibility criterion*, GM crops ought to be banned. However, the increased habitat loss and land conversion that would result from such a ban may be at least as irreversible, particularly if they lead to the extinction of species.

It is worth noting that the precautionary principle supports using terminator-type technology because that would minimize the possibility of gene transfer to weeds and non-GM plants without diminishing any of the public health or environmental benefits of GM crops. It is notable that some of the same groups that profess environmental concerns about genetic pollution have subjected terminator technology to unbridled criticism (Greenpeace 1998, FOE 1999b). In these groups' policy calculus, the potential environmental costs of GM crops are outweighed by the presumption that farmers will suffer economically because they will not be able to propagate GM crops from sterile seeds, and by antipathy toward multinationals' profits.

It is debatable whether putting antipathy to profits ahead of public health or the environment is any more commendable than putting profits ahead of them. It certainly does not advance either human or environmental well-being.

Would a Ban on GM Crops Further the Goals of the Convention on Biological Diversity?

The above analysis indicates that banning GM crops would more likely than not magnify threats to biodiversity and *in situ* conservation. But the preamble to the Convention on Biological Diversity (CBD) states that "it is vital to anticipate, prevent and attack the causes of significant reduction or loss of biological diversity at source" (Glowka et al. 1994: 10) and that "the fundamental requirement for the conservation of biological diversity is the in-situ conservation of ecosystems and natural habitats and the maintenance and recovery of viable populations of species in their natural surroundings" (Glowka et al. 1994: 11). Article 1 of the CBD also identifies as the first of its various objectives "the conservation of biological diversity." Thus, a ban on GM crops would be directly counter to the Convention's raison d'être.

Banning GM crops would also contradict the letter of the CBD. Article 8(d), which addresses *in situ* conservation, requires that "each contracting party shall, as far as possible and as appropriate . . . promote the protection of ecosystems, natural habitats and the maintenance of viable populations of species in natural surroundings" (Glowka et al. 1994: 39–41). A GM ban would also make it harder to satisfy the requirements of Article 8(a), which requires contracting parties to "establish a system of protected areas or areas where special measures need to be taken to conserve biological diversity" (Glowka et al. 1994: 39), because, as noted above, there would be less land and water available for *in situ* conservation, and what would be available would be socially and economically costlier to obtain and maintain (Goklany 1998a).

Would a Ban on GM Crops Advance the Goals of the Cartagena Biosafety Protocol?

Both the objective and scope of the Cartagena Biosafety Protocol (Articles 1 and 4, respectively) are specifically limited to GM organisms (GMOs) "that may have adverse effects on the conservation and sustainable use of biological diversity, taking also into account risks to human health" (CBD 2000). But we have seen that in the aggregate, by contrast with conventional crops, GM crops not only are unlikely to have adverse impacts on the environment, conservation, sustainable use, and human health but might result in net benefits. Thus, it can be argued that the case for a general ban on GM crops under the Protocol is, at best, weak. And it looks even weaker when one considers the sources of the Protocol's authorities.

As noted in its preamble and Article 1, the Protocol derives its authority regarding the regulation of the transfer, handling, and use of GMOs largely from Principle 15 of the Rio Declaration (UN 1992: 10), and Articles 17, 8(g), 19(3), and 19(4) of the CBD. Let's examine whether a general ban on GM crops would be supported under each of these sources of authority:

- Principle 15 of the Rio Declaration is a statement of the precautionary principle. But in previous sections we saw that the precautionary principle does not support a broad ban on GM crops.
- Article 17 of the CBD addresses only the facilitation of an exchange of information, so it cannot be used to justify a general ban on GM crops either.
- Article 8(g) of the CBD requires that contracting parties shall "establish or maintain means to regulate, manage or control the risks associated with the use and release of living modified organisms resulting from biotechnology which are likely to have adverse environmental impacts that could affect the conservation and sustainable use of biological diversity, taking also into account the risks to human health." This language parallels that in Articles 1 and 4 of the Protocol. The same rationale enunciated in the previous section applies to why it would be inappropriate to use that language to ban GM crops—namely, that GM crops in the aggregate are likely to have positive rather than adverse impact on conservation and sustainable use of biodiversity, and on human health.
- The same rationale explains why Article 19(3) of the CBD cannot be used to justify a GM crop ban. This Article requires that "the Parties shall consider the need for and modalities of a protocol setting out appropriate procedures, including, in particular, advance informed agreement, in the field of the safe transfer, handling and use of any living modified organism resulting from biotechnology that may have adverse effect on the conservation and sustainable use of biological diversity."
- Article 19(4) of the CBD operates only through Article 19(3) (Glowka et al. 1994: 97; CBD 2000). But, because Article 19(3) cannot justify a GM crop ban, neither can Article 19(4).

A counterargument could be made that the appropriate test to determine whether GM crops as a class should be subject to the Protocol's requirements would be to evaluate whether it may have *any*— and not just *aggregate*—adverse impact on the environment, conservation, sustainable use, and human health. However, as the *any* in Article 19(3) of the CBD indicates, the CBD's negotiators seem to have been cognizant of that word's significance: *any* appears 43 times in the Protocol (and 66 times in the Convention).

More importantly, had the CBD explicitly said *any* adverse impact, and had that then been used to impose a blanket ban on GM crops, it would have been counterproductive—and inconsistent with the goals of the Convention and the Protocol.

Conclusion

The precautionary principle has often been cited to justify a prohibition on GM crops (e.g., FOE 1999a, 1999b). However, that justification is based on a selective application of the principle to a limited set of consequences of such a policy. Specifically, the justification takes credit for the potential public health and environmental benefits of a ban on GM crops but refuses to accept responsibility for any concomitant risks that might be created or prolonged.

By comparison with conventional crops, GM crops would, in fact, increase the quantity and nutritional quality of food supplies and thereby improve public health by reducing mortality and morbidity rates worldwide. In addition, cultivation of GM rather than conventional crops would, by increasing productivity, reduce the amount of land and water that would otherwise have to be diverted to mankind's needs. GM crops could also reduce the environmental damage from the use of synthetic fertilizers and pesticides and from soil erosion. In comparison with conventional crops, GM crops would be more protective of habitat, biological diversity, air and water quality, carbon stores and sinks, and the world's atmosphere.

A ban on GM crops—whether accomplished directly by invoking the precautionary principle or indirectly via application(s) of the Biosafety Protocol—is likely to aggravate threats to biodiversity and further increase the already considerable hurdles facing *in situ* conservation. Therefore, a ban would be counterproductive and contravene the spirit and the letter of the CBD. The precautionary principle—properly applied, with a more comprehensive consideration of the public health and environmental consequences of a ban—argues instead for a sustained effort to research, develop, and commercialize GM crops, provided reasonable caution is exercised during testing and commercialization of the crops.

In this context, a "reasonable" precaution is one whose public health benefits are not negated by harmful reductions or delays in enhancing the quantity or quality of food. The public health costs of any reductions or delays—which would, at least for a period, make food more costly and reduce broader access to higher-quality food—would be disproportionately borne by the poorest and most vulnerable segments of society. In addition, the environmental gains flowing from a "reasonable" precaution should more than offset the environmental gains that would otherwise be obtained.

Notably, the Universal Declaration on Human Rights, passed by the United Nations General Assembly in 1948, recognizes the importance of adequate food, clothing, and housing. Article 25(1) states that "everyone has the right to a standard of living adequate for the health and well-being of himself and of his family, including food, clothing, housing. . .." (UN 1998). The Universal Declaration on the Eradication of Hunger and Malnutrition is much more explicit (UN 1974).[1] It specifies that "every man, woman and child has the inalienable right to be free from hunger and malnutrition." Thus, it could be argued that any efforts to block research, development, and, where appropriate, commercialization of GM crops would violate Article 10 of the Declaration on Human Rights, which states that "no one shall participate, by act or failure to act where required, in violating human rights and fundamental freedoms." (UN 1999).

In summary, the rewards of GM crops greatly outweigh their risks. Although it would be a mistake to go full steam ahead on GM crops, it would be a bigger mistake to stop them in their tracks. The wisest policy would be to go as fast as possible while keeping a sharp lookout, and staying on the track to improvements in human and environmental well-being. It could be argued that a policy that would ban GM crops would violate the basic human rights of hundreds of millions who are not yet free from hunger and malnutrition.

---

[1]Adopted on 16 November 1974 by the World Food Conference convened under General Assembly resolution 3180 (XXVIII) of December 17, 1973, and endorsed by General Assembly resolution 3348 (XXIX) of December 17, 1974.

4. Global Warming: From the Frying Pan into the Fire?

It was noted in Chapter 1 that the precautionary principle included in Article 3.3 of the United Nations Framework Convention on Climate Change apparently envisions using a global cost-benefit framework to design precautionary climate change measures (UN-FCCC 1992).[1] Despite Article 3.3 being an integral part of the UN-FCCC, more generic versions of the principle have sometimes been invoked as justification for going beyond "no regrets" actions[2] to address the potential threat of human-induced climate change (IPCC 1996a: 5; Perry 1999), which would reduce greenhouse gas (GHG) emissions beyond what might otherwise be achieved through secular (or normal) technological change or through reductions of economically inefficient subsidies. Under this argument, aggressive control of greenhouse gases is viewed as a precautionary measure similar to an insurance policy to forestall surprises or potentially disastrous consequences (Perry 1999).

Overlooked by this argument is the prospect that such an insurance policy itself might raise new—or aggravate existing—threats to human health or the environment (Cross 1998, Adler et al. 2000, Goklany 2000a). However, as we have seen in previous chapters, generic versions of the precautionary principle offer no guidance in instances in which a measure ostensibly designed to forestall uncertain public health and environmental problems might itself add to the world's health and environmental burden, thereby offsetting, if not negating, the presumed benefits of that measure.

In this chapter I use the framework presented in Chapter 1 to investigate whether it would be prudent to control GHGs beyond what would occur under "no regret" actions. In the parlance of the insurance metaphor, I would, in effect, undertake a qualitative cost-bene-

---

[1]This formulation does not necessarily call for the framework to be quantitative.

[2]"No regrets" actions are those that ought to be undertaken on their own merits, unrelated to any benefits related to global warming.

fit analysis of the insurance premium. That is what nearly all individuals or families do before purchasing insurance, whether it is for life, health, or property. And, of course, the amount of insurance purchased (if any) is affected by alternative uses for the funds. Instead of using dollars and cents, however, I will use a more qualitative assessment of the effects on public health and the environment as the basis for the cost-benefit calculus.

There is extensive and easily accessible literature concerning whether and why climate might have changed in the past century or so, and how much and how fast it might change in the future (see, e.g., IPCC 1996b, 2001a; Michaels and Balling 2000; Philander 2000; Singer 1998). Accordingly, I will not focus on those issues in detail here except to note that there is poor correspondence between temperature trends as measured by satellite, radiosonde, and surface instruments (IPCC 2001a: 2; World Climate Report 2001), and between trends in sea surface and air temperatures (Christy et al. 2001), neither of which has yet been resolved satisfactorily. These alternative data sets suggest that recent warming is less than reported by the IPCC (2001a: 1).

Some skeptics have also noted that global warming to date is substantially less than ought to have occurred if the estimates for the climate's sensitivity to GHG concentrations were accurate. To explain this discrepancy [see Michaels and Balling (2000) and IPCC (2001a) for the arguments], it has been suggested that some of the warming that ought to have occurred has been offset by cooling due to sulfates. Moreover, goes this counterargument, because developing countries are likely to impose more stringent SO_2 controls in the future (to reduce acidic deposition and sulfate formation), the sulfate cooling effect would be reduced, boosting future global warming (IPCC 2001a).

The latest chapter in this ongoing argument is a recent study by Jacobson (2001) suggesting that past sulfate cooling should have been offset by greater heat absorption by dark soot formed during combustion of fossil fuels and forests worldwide. If that is indeed the case, we are back to where we started, that is, the models overestimate climate sensitivity to GHG buildup. A recent paper by Lindzen et al. (2001) gives greater credence to the contention that the treatment of clouds in present models is flawed and significantly overestimates warming. Lindzen's paper, based on satellite measurements over the tropical Pacific Ocean, indicates that as the ocean warms the areal extent of cirrus clouds relative to cumulus clouds declines, which allows more heat to escape into the upper atmosphere, cooling the surface. In other words, cirrus clouds over the oceans seem to act as a thermostat. No such mechanism is built into current models.

However, instead of dealing with the issues surrounding the physics of climate change, the following discussion focuses on the *impact* of climate change on the basis that the fundamental reason why climate change is on the international policy agenda is not climate change per se but its impact. In fact, if climate were to change but have no impact, climate change would merely be a scientific curiosity worth investigating in its own right, but not a public policy issue (Goklany 1992). In the rest of this chapter I also address the potential impacts of climate change over the next several decades, rather than impacts that might occur after centuries or millennia of sustained, and drastic, climate change, such as collapse of the West Antarctic ice sheet or the shutting down of the thermohaline circulation in the North Atlantic (IPCC 2001a: 10–11).

At the time of this writing, the IPCC's full Third Assessment Report (TAR) had not yet been released; therefore, the projections of the impacts of climate change provided here are based on the IPCC's Second Assessment Report (SAR) (IPCC 1996a, 1996b, 1996c). Although press reports have highlighted the statement from the IPCC Work Group I's latest *Summary for Policymakers* that the upper limit to the range of future climate change projections in 2100 has increased to 5.8°C (IPCC 2001a: 8), they have overlooked the fact that the same report on the same page goes on to state as follows:

> On timescales of a few decades, the current observed rate of warming can be used to constrain the projected response to a given emissions scenario despite uncertainty in climate sensitivity. This approach suggests that anthropogenic warming is likely to lie in the range of 0.1 to 0.2°C per decade over the next few decades.

In other words, if one accepts that recent trend data from surface temperature measurements are valid—a proposition that many skeptics have challenged—then, according to the TAR itself, the likely change in temperature for the next few decades is not much different from what was estimated in the SAR. In fact the TAR notes that climate sensitivity to an equivalent doubling of GHGs has not changed much, and that the new estimate for rising sea levels

(0.09–0.88 meters, or 4–35 inches) is marginally lower than that contained in the SAR (0.13–0.94 meters, or 5–37 inches) (IPCC 2001a: 10). Thus, the "likely" estimates of climate change impacts over the next few decades should be based on scenarios that correspond to globally averaged temperature changes of 0.1–0.2°C per decade. In fact, the scenarios used in most studies reported in the SAR exceeded that range (Goklany 1998b, 2000a). The conclusions of the TAR with respect to future impacts seem to be qualitatively similar to those in the SAR, except that they seem more upbeat about the timber supply increasing as a result of climate change (IPCC 2001b: 4).

Net Impacts of Uncontrolled Global Warming

The net global and regional impacts of human-induced climate change (or global warming) are inherently uncertain because projections of future impacts are based on a series of model calculations in which each succeeding model uses as its inputs increasingly uncertain outputs of the previous model (Goklany 1992, 1995a, 2000a; IPCC 1996c).

First, future emissions of GHGs must be estimated by using uncertain projections of future population, economic conditions, energy use, land use, and land cover. These emissions are themselves sensitive to climatic conditions and to atmospheric concentrations. Second, these emissions have to be converted into each GHG's atmospheric concentration. Third, these concentrations have to be used to determine future "radiation forcing," which is then used (ideally) by coupled atmospheric and ocean models to project climatic changes (such as changes in seasonal temperatures and precipitation, seasonal highs and lows, and changes in diurnal variability).

Because geography itself is an important determinant of the climate, climatic changes should be estimated at relatively fine geographical scales. Moreover, the distribution and abundance of natural resources, which are the basis of most climate-sensitive natural and human systems, are spatially heterogeneous. But regardless of how much confidence one may have in the ability of climate models to estimate globally averaged climatic changes, the finer the geographic scale, the more uncertain the results.

These uncertain location-specific climatic changes serve as inputs to simplified and often inadequate models that project location-spe-

60

cific biophysical changes (e.g., crop or timber yields). Then, depending on the human or natural system under consideration, the outputs of these biophysical models may have to be fed into additional models to calculate impacts on those systems. For example, estimates of crop yields in specific areas should serve as inputs for a model of the global agricultural system in order to estimate the overall impact on food security.

Ideally, there ought to be dynamic feedback loops between several of the models in the entire chain of models going from emissions to impact estimates. For instance, the climate affects photosynthesis and respiration on the earth's surface which, in turn, affects global CO_2 emissions. Therefore, there ought to be dynamic feedbacks from the impact and climate models to the emissions models. But to ease calculations, those feedback loops are generally ignored or replaced by static inputs or "boundary" conditions.

Thus, estimates of the impacts of global warming in any specific location at any particular time are probably even more uncertain than estimates of globally averaged temperature and/or precipitation. Moreover, net global impacts—because they are an aggregation of the various location-specific impacts—are also uncertain, although there may be some cancellation of errors. Nonetheless, the uncertainties are large enough that one cannot be confident of the magnitude or, in many cases, even the direction of impacts—that is, whether the net impacts are positive or negative. This is true not only for specific geographic locations but also globally.

Moreover, for climate-sensitive systems or indicators that are affected by human actions (e.g., agriculture, forests, land use, land cover, habitat loss, and biodiversity), impact models should include socioeconomic models, which ought to—but often do not—fully incorporate secular changes in technology and "automatic" adaptations, among other things. Failure to reasonably account for such technological change and human adaptability results in a substantial upward bias in the projected negative consequences of climatic change. Human ingenuity not only can mitigate adverse effects but also can harness positive consequences of climate change. The forecasting landscape is strewn with spectacular duds that have failed to account for this factor, including the Club of Rome's *Limits to Growth*, the Carter Administration's *Global 2000* report, and Paul Ehrlich's *The Population Bomb* (Frederick et al. 1994; Goklany 1992, 1996, 2000a).

Regardless of the uncertainties about impacts, unless fossil fuel emissions from both developed and developing countries are curtailed drastically, a number of developments are likely.

- *Atmospheric carbon dioxide concentrations will most likely continue to rise.* All else being equal, higher carbon dioxide concentrations mean greater productivity for agriculture, if not vegetation in general (IPCC 1996c, Idso and Idso 2000, Wittwer 1995). And greater agricultural productivity means more food, which leads to better nutrition, which, in turn, ought to result in better health, less disease, and lower mortality (Goklany 1999a, 2001a). The remarkable increases in global agricultural productivity and global food supplies per capita since the end of World War II—despite a much larger population—have been accompanied by substantial worldwide improvements in health, reductions in mortality rates, and increases in life expectancies (Goklany 1998a, 1999a, 2001a). Most of the credit for these achievements is generally assigned to agricultural, medical, and public health technologies and practices, economic development (which makes more productive and improved technologies more affordable), and trade (which moves food surpluses to food deficit areas and generally stimulates both economic growth and diffusion of technology) (Goklany 1995a, 1998a, 1998b, 1999c, 1999d). Nevertheless, some credit is due to the past increase in CO_2 concentrations and, perhaps, to any associated global warming (Wittwer 1995, Nicholls 1997, Goklany 1998b).
- *Globally averaged temperatures will be higher, but the degree of warming and its geographic distribution are uncertain.* There ought to be greater warming in the higher latitudes, at night, and during the winter. In general this means, among other things, greater agricultural and forest productivity in the higher latitudes because of longer growing seasons, but it could increase heat stress and reduce productivity in the tropics (Goklany 1992, IPCC 1996c). Although the contribution of warming per se to the historical increases in global agricultural productivity is not yet known, growing seasons and forest productivity have been increasing in the northern latitudes, perhaps because of a combination of higher nighttime temperatures during the winter and higher CO_2 concentrations (Myneni et al. 1997, Tans and White 1998, Fan et al. 1998, Tian et al. 1998). Similarly, Magnuson et al.

(2000) find that freeze dates for river and lake ice seem to be occurring an average of 5.8 days later than they did 150 years ago, and thawing dates are occurring an average of 6.5 days earlier than they did 100 years ago.

- *Globally averaged precipitation may increase, although precipitation may decline in some areas.* The timing of rainfall also may be altered. More precipitation does not necessarily translate into greater availability of moisture for growing crops and vegetation. In some areas, increased evaporation caused by higher temperatures may, all else being equal, more than offset increased precipitation. On the other hand, the water use efficiency of vegetation improves with increasing carbon dioxide concentrations. Thus, it is very difficult to predict the amount of water needed to grow specific crops and other vegetation at any given location (IPCC 1996c; IPCC 2001a: 8).

- *Although there has been no discernible increase in the rate at which sea levels have risen over the past century as a result of global warming, it could conceivably accelerate in the future* (IPCC 1996b; IPCC 2001a: 6).

- *Altered patterns of temperature and precipitation combined with increasing CO_2 concentrations will cause some animal and vegetation species to migrate.* The ensemble of species or the "ecosystem" at any specific location today will thus be altered, as will the abundance of individual species at that location (Goklany 1992, 1995a; IPCC 1996c: 451–454; IPCC 2001a: 8). But whether these changes constitute a net benefit or loss is unclear. Not only is the "final" distribution of species uncertain; there are also no criteria for establishing whether the change has resulted in a net loss or benefit to humanity or to the rest of nature. Proponents of GHG controls implicitly assume that any change is inherently detrimental, but that is more an article of faith than the product of a rational inquiry into aspects such as changes in net or gross productivity, or the mix and abundance of species.

In addition, the potential spread of vector-borne diseases in a warmer world has been raised as one of the major concerns regarding anthropogenic climate change. Some fear that vectors such as the anopheles mosquito, the carrier of malaria, could become more widespread with warming because a change in climate could alter the range and abundance of species (McMichael et al. 1996a, 1996b).

Malaria was estimated to have killed 1.1 million people in 1999 (WHO 2000). However, historical data indicate that the prevalence of these diseases depends less on their potential ranges than on an understanding of their causes and the public health measures taken to deal with the vectors and the diseases they spread. In fact, a recent National Academy of Sciences report notes that for such reasons the "impact of climate change on human health is 'highly uncertain'" (*National Academies News* 2001, based on National Research Council 2001).

Malaria, cholera, and other diarrheal and parasitic diseases that were prevalent around the world during the last century, including in the United States and Western Europe, have been rolled back around the world (Howard 1909; Porter 1996; Goklany 1999d; Reiter 1996, 2000). Few recognize the toll these diseases took in the 19th century in today's developed countries. For instance, mainly because of cholera, yellow fever, typhoid, and various diarrheal and gastrointestinal diseases, the mean crude death rate (CDR) in New Orleans for a 30-year period between 1830 and 1859 was 60,000 per million (Smillie 1952). By comparison, in 1990–95, it was 44,600 per million for Rwanda—the nation with the world's highest crude death rate—and 8,800 for the United States (WRI 1998). In 1900, the cumulative death rate in the United States for typhoid, paratyphoid, various gastrointestinal diseases, and all forms of dysentery was 1,860 per million population (Goklany 1996). Today, due to a host of public health measures, those diseases barely show up in current U.S. statistics, accounting for a death rate of less than 5 per million (Rosenberg et al. 1996).

Thus, despite any warming that may have occurred, advances and investments in, and greater availability of, food, nutrition, medicine, and public health technology helped reduce infectious and parasitic diseases worldwide, particularly among the young in developing countries. As a result, crude global death rate has dropped, which has pushed global life expectancy at birth from 46.4 in 1950–55 to 64.3 years in 1990–95 (WRI 1998, Goklany 2001a). Today, climate-sensitive infectious and parasitic diseases are problems only where the necessary public health measures are unaffordable or have been compromised (Goklany 1999d, 2000a; Reiter 1996, 2000; Bryan et al. 1996).

It has been suggested that climate change may be a factor in the recent resurgences in vector-borne diseases in some parts of the globe

(McMichael 1996a, 1996b), including malaria in Henan Province (China), malaria and dengue fever in the Americas, and cholera in Peru and Rwanda. More likely causes, however, appear to be increases in drug resistance; increased urbanization that can lead to unsanitary conditions that facilitate the spread of infectious diseases; premature discontinuation of control measures such as indoor spraying and use of impregnated mosquito nets; and faltering mosquito control and public health measures (e.g., reduced use of DDT and chlorination), aggravated by poor nutrition (Taubes 1997; Pinheiro and Chuit 1998; Sleigh et al. 1998; Besser et al. 1995; Roberts et al. 1997, 2000b; Goklany 2000a). In many developing countries, malaria has retreated, then advanced and, in some places, retreated once again as in-home malaria spraying was increased, then decreased, then increased again (Roberts et al. 1997, 2000b; see Chapter 2).

Although extreme temperatures pose less serious public health problems than infectious and parasitic diseases, they too are a source of concern for public health because extreme heat (as well as extreme cold) can lead to death and sickness (McMichael et al. 1996a; Kilbourne 1997a, 1997b). Gaffen and Ross (1998) reported that between 1949 and 1995 the frequency of "extreme heat stress events" increased in the United States. They suggested that continuation of this trend could pose public health problems in the future. However, an analysis by Goklany and Straja (2000) of death certificate data from the Centers for Disease Control and Prevention (CDC 2000b) shows no upward trends in U.S. crude death rates caused by either excessive heat or excessive cold between 1979 and 1997, despite the aging of the population (Goklany and Straja 2000). One explanation for the lack of a trend is that technological changes might have overwhelmed any increased risks arising from meteorological changes.

Despite the uncertainties associated with the impacts of climate change and the previously noted tendency to systematic overestimation of negative impacts,[3] I assume here that, by and large, the SAR's assessment of the future impacts of global warming is relatively sound. The IPCC estimates suggest that in the absence of further GHG controls, over the next several decades the net impacts of global warming will be relatively small compared with other envi-

---

[3]At the same time, by not properly accounting for technological change, these studies also underestimate the ability to take advantage of positive impacts.

ronmental and natural resource problems facing the globe (see Table 4-1) (Goklany 1998b, 1999a, 2000a).

In the absence of warming, global agricultural production would have to increase 83 percent between 1990 and 2060 to meet additional food demand from a larger and richer global population, according to one study relied upon by the IPCC's SAR (Reilly et al. 1996, Rosenzweig and Parry 1994). Global warming may decrease production in developing countries but increase it in developed nations, resulting in a net change in global production of $+1$ or -2 percent in 2060.

It should be noted that the Rosenzweig and Parry study used a globally averaged temperature change for 2060 that was higher than the IPCC's "best estimate" for 2100 (Goklany 1998b, 2000a). It also considered only a few of the potential adaptations that could be available in 2060 (or, for that matter, 2100). For instance, it did not consider the potential for productivity-enhancing techniques such as development of cultivars that can better tolerate drought, salt, and acidic conditions and that can better take advantage of higher atmospheric CO_2 concentrations. These technologies are merely gleams in our eyes today but could be realities six decades from now, perhaps as a result of bioengineering (see Chapter 3). On the other hand, the analysis did not consider any change in the proportion of crops lost to insects and other pests. Of course, crop protection is an ongoing challenge for farmers everywhere with or without climate change (Goklany 1998a, 1999c, 2000a).

Even without global warming, greater agricultural and other human demands may reduce forest cover by 25 percent or more by 2050, putting enormous pressure on the world's biodiversity (IPCC 1996c: 95–129, 492–96). However, global warming alone—ignoring the beneficial effects of CO_2 on photosynthesis and water-use efficiency—may actually *increase* forest cover by 1 to 9 percent (IPCC 1996c: 95–129, 492–96). The existing boundaries of current forest types would almost certainly shift poleward. A priori, there is no reason to believe this would lead to a diminution of global biological diversity in terms of the number of species or their abundance. It is worth noting that wetter and warmer climatic conditions often seem to harbor greater biodiversity, as long as sufficient water is available (Hawksworth et al. 1995, Huston 1994).

By 2100, the incidence of malaria (which may be thought of as a metaphor for climate-sensitive infectious and parasitic diseases) may

Table 4-1

Projected Climate Change Impacts With and Without the Kyoto Protocol vs. Other Environmental Problems

Climate-Sensitive Sector/ Indicator	Year	Baseline including Impacts of Environmental Problems Other than Climate Change	Impact/Effect	
			Impacts of Climate Change, on Top of Baseline Without Kyoto Protocol	*Impacts of Kyoto Protocol Relative to Baseline**
Agricultural production	2060 for socio-economic baseline >2100 for climate change	Must increase 83% relative to 1990	Net global production would change −2.4% to +1.1% but could substantially redistribute production from developing to developed countries	Net global production would change −0.2% to +0.1%
Global forest area	2050	Decrease 25–30(+)%, relative to 1990	Increase in global forest area of at least 1%–9%	Reduce the *increase* in global forest area
Malaria incidence	2060	500 million	25 to 40 million additional cases	Reduction in number of cases by 0.5%–0.8%
	2100	500 million	50 to 80 million additional cases	Reduction in number of cases by 1%–1.6%
Sea level rise (SLR)	2060	Varies	~25 cm (or 10 inches)	Reduce SLR by 1 inch
	2100	Varies	~50 cm (or 20 inches)	Reduce SLR by 2 inches
Extreme weather events	2060 or 2100	Unknown	Unknown whether magnitudes or frequencies of occurrence will increase or decrease in any specific area	Unknown

Source: Goklany (1998b, 2000a), based on IPCC (1996b, 1996c).
* Assumes that the Kyoto Protocol, if implemented, would reduce climate change and its impacts by 10 percent (see the text).

increase by about 10 to 16 percent of the base rate in the absence of warming (IPCC 1996c: 561–84). The increase may be half that in 2060 (Goklany 1999d, 2000a). Although these increases are small compared with the baseline rate, they are likely to be overestimates because the analysis is based on the notion that warming will expand the geographical ranges of the responsible vectors. That theory has been disputed by some authorities on tropical diseases (Reiter 1996, Dye and Reiter 2000, Bryan et al. 1996, Taubes 1997, Rogers and Randolph 2000), who note that the range of vectors depends not only on temperature extremes, but also, among other things, on the timing, quantity, and seasonality of precipitation and runoff.

Perhaps more importantly, the current ranges of these diseases seem to be dictated less by climate than by human adaptability (Goklany 1998b, 2000a; Reiter 2000; Dye and Reiter 2000; Rogers and Randolph 2000; NRC 2001). In fact, despite the global warming that is supposed to have taken place over the past century (or more), many of the once-deadliest infectious and parasitic diseases (e.g., malaria, yellow fever, and cholera) have been virtually eradicated in richer countries like the United States and Italy where they were once prevalent. That has happened because, in general, a wealthier society has better nutrition, better general health, and greater access to public health measures and technologies targeted at controlling disease (Goklany 1992, 1995a, 1999a, 2000a, 2001a). Given improvements in public health measures and technologies that ought to occur in the next several decades with the rapid expansion in our knowledge of diseases and the development of institutions devoted to health and medical research, the importance of climate in determining the ranges of these diseases is likely to diminish further. Despite all these considerations, I have assumed in Table 4-1 that the estimates of 5–8 percent by 2050 or 10–16 percent by 2100 are robust.

Although there has not been any discernible increase in the rate of sea level rise over the past century, sea levels may rise 3 to 19 inches by 2060 (with a "best estimate" of 10 inches), and about twice that by 2100 (Warrick et al. 1996). The global cost estimate for protecting against a 20-inch rise in 2100 is about $1 billion per year (Pearce et al. 1996), or less than 0.005 percent of global economic product (Goklany 2000a).

Proponents of limits on GHG emissions have also speculated that the frequency and intensity of extreme weather events may be increased by global warming, as would deaths and damages caused by such events. But so far there seems to be little evidence of that (IPCC 2001a: 3, 9). In fact, despite any increased global warming during the past century, U.S. data show that in the past decades, death rates attributable to hurricanes, floods, tornadoes, and lightning have declined 60 to 99 percent since their peaks (based on 9-year moving averages, see Figure 4-1) (Goklany 1998b, 2000a). In addition, although U.S. property losses from floods and hurricanes increased somewhat in terms of "real" dollars during the 20th century, because an increasingly larger and richer population had more property at risk, losses did not increase in terms of percentage of wealth (Figures 4-2 and 4-3) (Goklany 1998b, 2000a). Finally, there seems to be little scientific basis for concluding that in the future ex-

FIGURE 4-1
DEATH RATES DUE TO TORNADOS, FLOODS, LIGHTNING, AND
HURRICANES, (PER MILLION POPULATION, 9-YEAR MOVING
AVERAGES, 1900 TO 1997)

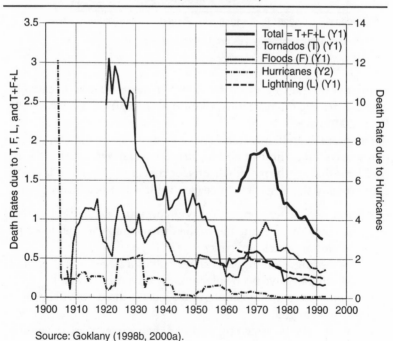

Source: Goklany (1998b, 2000a).

FIGURE 4-2
PROPERTY LOSSES DUE TO FLOODS, 1903 TO 1997

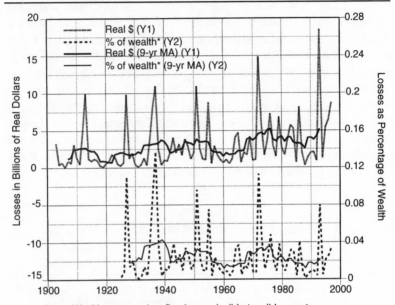

Note: Wealth measured as fixed reproducible tangible assets.

Source: Goklany (1998b, 2000a).

treme events will be more frequent or more intense because of global warming (Henderson-Sellers et al. 1998; IPCC 1996b: 332–35; IPCC 2001a: 3, 9).

Therefore, stabilizing GHG concentrations immediately, even if feasible, would do little or nothing *over the next several decades* to solve problems that are the major reasons for concern about warming—except possibly rising sea level rise (see Table 4-1). Specifically:

- Land and water conversion will continue virtually unabated, with little or no reduction in the threats to forests, biodiversity, and carbon stores and sinks.
- The feeding, clothing, and sheltering of a larger world population will not have been substantially advanced, if at all.
- Incidence rates of infectious and parasitic diseases will be virtually unchanged.
- Poorer nations, which by virtue of their poverty are deemed to be most vulnerable to the adverse impacts of climate change,

Global Warning: From the Frying Pan into the Fire?

will continue to be vulnerable to all kinds of adversity, natural and manmade.

Thus, while global warming may be a serious problem in the long run, other environmental and health problems are likely to be much more urgent for the next several decades (Goklany 1998b, 2000a).

Net Impacts of Aggressively Forcing the Pace of GHG Emission Reductions

One approach to reducing GHGs would be to let secular techno-logical change run its course. In due time, that might reduce GHG emissions. Carbon intensities of currently developed countries (in

FIGURE 4-3
HURRICANE PROPERTY LOSSES, 1900 TO 1997

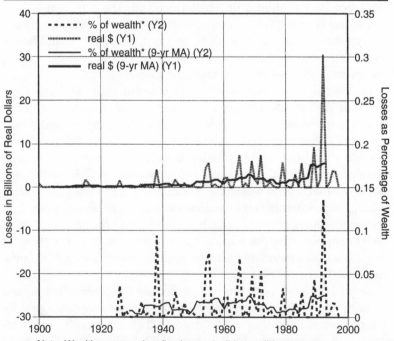

Note: Wealth measured as fixed reproducible tangible assets.
Source: Goklany (1998b, 2000a).

71

terms of CO_2 emissions per GDP) have declined 1.3 percent per year since 1850 (Nakicenovic et al. 1998). Based on this century-and-a-half trend and the variety of technical options available for providing energy services, Ausubel (1998a) and Nakicenovic et al. (1998) suggest that economies will probably continue to decarbonize. Options include increased use of natural gas, nuclear energy, renewable energy sources, fuel cells, and greater conservation.

But it takes more than the availability of technology to create technological change. It also takes financial means and institutional support (Goklany 1992, 1995a, 1998a, 1999b). Fiscal resources for implementation will have to be generated through economic growth. The higher the rate of economic growth, the higher the rate of decarbonization of an economy (Nakicenovic et al. 1998). However, it is possible that without additional stimulus, the rate of economic growth will outstrip the rate of secular decarbonization of the economy, and CO_2 emissions might never stabilize.

Accordingly, proponents of GHG controls argue that the pace of decarbonization should be accelerated. But the question is how much and how fast GHG emissions should be reduced, who should reduce them, how they should be reduced, and what would be the impacts of any reduction requirements on global society and the global economy and on the rate of climate change.

For instance, we could stabilize CO_2 concentrations at current levels—but that would require immediate emission reductions of *at least* 50 percent because about 50 percent of the anthropogenic emissions of CO_2 are absorbed by the oceans and on land (IPCC 2001a: 4). Like it or not, the world is fueled largely by carbon-based energy sources. Therefore, the social and economic costs of GHG reductions of such a magnitude would be prohibitively high, unless one were willing to assume decarbonization rates substantially greater than historically have been the case. In recognition of this, proponents of GHG controls argue for implementing a more modest first step, to serve as a down payment for wider and deeper emissions cuts down the road (Warrick 1998).

Requiring developing countries to reduce GHG emissions would be particularly devastating to their prospects for economic growth, which is essential if they are to improve their lot socially, economically, and environmentally (Goklany 1992, 1995a, 2001a). To shield the developing world from the high costs associated with GHG reductions, it has been suggested that, at least initially, GHG control requirements should be restricted to developed countries. The energy infrastructure of developing countries is not only substantially more inefficient than that of developed countries, but it is also in greater need of expansion, and it makes sense to ensure that new capacity uses more efficient technology. Thus, it has been argued, it would be cheaper overall if developed countries discharged their "obligations" to reduce GHG emissions (or at least a portion of them) by paying for clean energy technologies in developing countries. Such transfer payments could be, it has been argued, justified under the emissions trading concept.

All of these considerations were brought together in the Kyoto Protocol, negotiated in December 1997 by the Conference of the Parties to the United Nations Framework Convention on Climate Change (UNFCCC 1992). The Protocol requires 38 developed countries (including the United States) to reduce CO_2 emissions by 2008–12 to an average of 5.2 percent below their 1990 levels. But it does not specify any targets or timetables for developing countries. That is one of the reasons why the U.S. Senate seems unlikely to ratify it soon. More importantly, the Protocol would reduce the amount of climatic change by 2100 by 3–10 percent at most (Masood 1997; Wigley 1998, 1999; Malakoff 1997; Parry 2000). This modest reduction—probably within the noise level of natural variability—is a consequence of the inertia of the climate system, the Protocol's limited geographic coverage, and the fact that much of the future growth in GHG emissions is expected to occur in exactly those countries to which the Protocol would give a bye—that is, developing countries.

Let us assume that the Kyoto Protocol would reduce the amount of climate change by 10 percent, which is at the high end of what is expected to occur by 2100 if the Protocol is implemented. Let us further assume, as an approximation, that would translate into a reduction in the *impacts* of climate change in each of the climate-sensitive sectors or indicators by 10 percent.[4] Then according to the last column in Table 4-1, full implementation of the Kyoto Protocol would,

---

[4]If one assumes that the impacts of climate change [$I(\theta)$] as a function of global temperature (θ) can be represented by a Taylor series, then this approximation would be valid at least to the first order because the temperature change ($\Delta\theta$) due to human-induced climate change is small relative to the "natural" temperature (θ_0). See, for example, Goldstein et al. (1999).

over the next few decades, only marginally improve human or environmental well-being.

For instance, instead of the 550 million to 580 million potential cases of malaria in 2100 (of which 500 million would occur even if climate were not to change), there would be 545 million to 572 million cases. Such a relatively small reduction—1 to 2 percent of total projected malaria incidence in 2100—might be justifiable if the costs were minor and if other, more effective opportunities for improving human and environmental well-being were all used up. But the cost of Kyoto, which its advocates conceive to be only a small down payment toward much more deeper reductions in the future, is estimated to be in the hundreds of billions of dollars. An analysis done by MIT's Joint Program on the Science and Policy of Global Change (2000) estimates that in 2010, depending on the extent of emissions trading, the Protocol would cost between $90 billion and $116 billion (in 1995 U.S. dollars). About 50 percent of those costs would be borne by the United States. Another analysis done by the Department of Energy in 1998 estimates that U.S. annual gross domestic product would be lowered by $56 billion to $437 billion in 2010 (in 1992 dollars) (EIA 1998).

To put these costs into context, consider that according to the World Health Organization, a life could be saved from malaria at a cost of $750-$2,500 (WHO 1999a: 56). The World Health Organization also estimates that annual expenditures of between $375 million and $1.25 billion could halve malaria's death toll of about 1.1 million per year (WHO 1999a: 56).

Table 4-1 indicates that the global benefits of the Kyoto Protocol in terms of reducing impacts on other climate-sensitive sectors and indicators will be quite modest, perhaps within the noise level, for the next several decades.

In addition, even if the relatively large transfer payments that developed countries might make to developing countries under the guise of emissions trading actually materialize—and there is no guarantee they will, because the populations of the developed countries are not necessarily predisposed to such payments—the economies of the poorer countries would not be fully shielded from the adverse impacts of the costs of the Protocol on the richer countries. This is because a significant portion of developing countries' economic output depends on their trade with developed countries.

In 1995–97, exports accounted for 17.9 and 24.5 percent of the GDPs of the low- and medium-income countries, respectively (World Bank 1999). The corresponding figures in 1990–92 were 14.2 and 21.7 percent; that is, in the intervening five years, the share of GDP attributable to exports rose 26 and 13 percent, respectively. The rise was even more rapid for the least-developed countries—37 percent (from 13.1 to 17.9 percent of GDP). An analysis done during the earlier period indicated that a 1 percent drop in the GDP of developed countries translated into a $60 billion loss in the exports of developing countries (World Bank 1992; Goklany 1995a). It would undoubtedly be a larger figure today if adjustments were made for increased trade and inflation. Thus, some developing countries—particularly those that might not receive sufficient transfer funds—might have lower levels of economic development because of the Kyoto Protocol, as would many of the developed countries targeted by the Protocol.

It is critical to recognize that economic development is not an end in itself but provides the means to other worthy ends, including the improvement of human well-being and the environment. Virtually every indicator of human well-being improves with the level of economic development (Goklany 1992, 1999a, 2000a, 2001a). Wealth created, which helps to increase food supplies per capita (Figure 4-4),[5] which in turn reduces hunger and malnutrition. Economic development also makes basic public health services more available. Working together, improved health services and higher food supplies help reduce mortality rates. Thus, as levels of economic development increase, mortality rates decline and life expectancies increase, as we saw in Figures 2-1 and 2-2.

Figures 2-1 and 2-2 show that improvements are most rapid at the lowest levels of economic development, that is, a uniformly small de-

---

[5]The smoothed curve in Figure 4-4, taken from Goklany (2001a), is fitted using a log-linear model. In this and subsequent figures, GDP per capita (or per capita income) is given in 1995 U.S. dollars based on the market exchange rate (MXR). $N = 150$ and $R^2 = 0.63$. The slope is significant at the 0.001 level. The scale on the x-axis is cut off at a GDP per capita of $10,000 to better illustrate the rapid change in available food supplies per capita per day at low levels of per capita income. The y-axis scale commences at 1,500 kilocalories/capita/day in recognition of the fact that the minimum energy needed by the body to perform basic activities at rest in a supine position is in the general range of 1,300 to 1,700 kcals/day for adults with different characteristics (i.e., age, sex, height, body weight).

FIGURE 4-4
AVAILABLE FOOD SUPPLY VS. GDP PER CAPITA, 1994

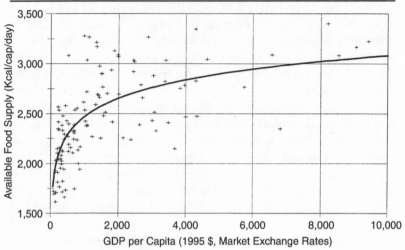

GDP per Capita (1995 $, Market Exchange Rates)

Source: Goklany (2000b).

cline in incomes will have a larger negative impact in developing countries than it will in richer countries. Thus, aggressively forcing the pace of reductions could increase mortality rates and lower life expectancies, particularly in the developing countries (see also Cross 1998). Those costs would be only partially balanced, if at all, by the more speculative benefits associated with a reduction in the impacts of reduced warming, which, moreover, are more distant in time.

Reduced economic development has other downsides from the perspective of public health and environmental quality. First, lower levels of economic development are correlated with higher total fertility rates (see Figure 4-5),[6] which tends to push up population growth rates (Goklany 1992, 1995a, 1999a, 2000a).

Second, it diminishes a society's adaptability to adversity, in general, and to climate change in particular (Goklany 1992, 1995a, 1999a, 2000a). Poorer societies have fewer resources available to research, develop, acquire, operate, and maintain technologies that would

[6]The smoothed curve in Figure 4-5, taken from Goklany (2000b), is fitted using a log-linear relationship. N and R^2 are 148 and 0.55, respectively. The slope is significant at the 0.001 level. The x-axis scale is cut off at $20,000 per capita.

FIGURE 4-5
TOTAL FERTILITY RATE VS. GDP PER CAPITA, 1997

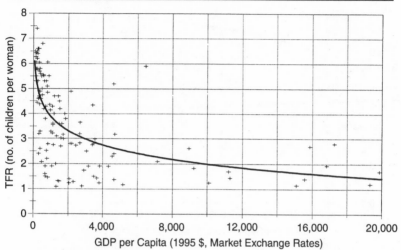

GDP per Capita (1995 $, Market Exchange Rates)
Source: Goklany (2000b).

help society better cope with whatever problems it may be plagued with, including unmet public health, environmental, and social needs. Richer societies are better able to afford the higher levels of education that help create and maintain human capital, and human capital is a prerequisite for bringing about and implementing beneficial changes in technologies (Goklany 2001a). Thus, it is no surprise that access to safe water and sanitation increases with the level of economic development. Figure 4-6,[7] for instance, shows that access to safe water increases with economic development and that, once again, improvement is most rapid at the lowest levels of development (Goklany 2001a).

Third, a poorer society has lower crop yields (see Figure 4-7, for cereals).[8] For any specific level of crop production, more habitat and

[7]The smoothed curve in Figure 4-6 is taken from Goklany (2000b), N is 51 for 1995. Because a number of countries were already at 100 percent in 1995, a Tobit model was used for truncation at that level. The untruncated log-linear regression had R^2 of 0.55 for 1995. The slope is significant at the 0.001 level. This figure presents the data up to $20,000.

[8]The smoothed curve in Figure 4-7 is fitted using a log-linear relationship (Goklany 2000b). N and R^2 are 138 and 0.49, respectively. The slope is significant at the 0.001 level.

FIGURE 4-6
ACCESS TO SAFE WATER VS. GDP PER CAPITA, 1995

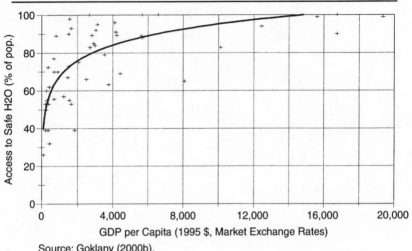

GDP per Capita (1995 $, Market Exchange Rates)

Source: Goklany (2000b).

FIGURE 4-7
CEREAL YIELD VS. GDP PER CAPITA, 1997

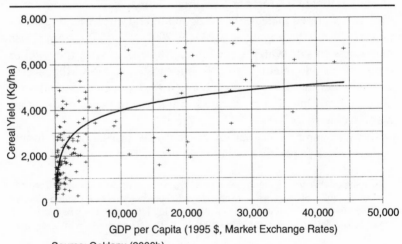

GDP per Capita (1995 $, Market Exchange Rates)

Source: Goklany (2000b).

forest land have to be converted to cropland to compensate for lower yields. This puts greater pressure on biodiversity and reduces carbon stores and sinks. In fact, such conversion is the major threat to global biodiversity (Goklany 1992, 1995a, 1998a; Wilcove et al. 1998). As was noted previously, it is hardly surprising that between 1980 and 1995 forest cover in developing countries decreased by 190 million hectares (Mha) while it increased by 20 million hectares in the developed countries (FAO 1997). Finally, efforts to substantially reduce GHG emissions could, over the next several decades, divert scarce resources from more urgent environmental and public health problems, such as control of malaria or other climate-sensitive infectious or parasitic diseases (see Table 4-1).

As we have seen, future environmental and public health problems unrelated to climate change should substantially outweigh the adverse impacts of climate change for the next several decades. Thus, it would be counterproductive if, in the quest to make it easier to cope with the future adverse effects of climate change, we compromised the ability to cope with current public health and environmental problems that are more urgent today and are likely to remain so over the next few decades (Goklany 2000a).

As an alternative to accelerating secular (i.e., ongoing long-term) trends that would reduce GHG emissions, energy prices could be increased through taxes or through elimination of subsidies. Such price increases, however, could have unintended consequences.

First, the productivity of the agriculture sector would be reduced because that sector is heavily dependent on oil and gas for running its farm machinery, producing inputs such as fertilizers and pesticides, powering irrigation systems, and moving outputs from farm to market. Thus, food production would decline or prices would rise, or both. This is precisely what happened following the oil shocks of the 1970s (Pinstrup-Andersen et al. 1999: 21, Figure 4). In either case, food would be less accessible to those who were less well off, and hunger and malnutrition would increase, which, in turn, would probably increase rates of death and disease among those groups.

Second, an estimated 2.8 million people worldwide die annually because of indoor air pollution, mainly because of the burning of solid fuels (e.g., coal, wood, and dung) for heating and cooking in the home (WHO 1997a). Increasing fossil fuel prices would only make it harder for households using solid fuels to switch to cleaner, commercial fossil fuels.

Third, increasing fuel prices would inhibit the operation of heaters in the winter and air conditioners in the summer, which could lead to greater sickness, if not mortality, caused by cold and heat waves (Goklany and Straja 2000).

Applying the Precautionary Principle to Global Warming

The above analysis indicates that forcing the pace of GHG controls over the next several decades could indirectly aggravate hunger and reduce public health services, either of which, separately or together, could increase mortality, particularly in developing countries. On the other hand, such a policy might reduce the putative public health and environmental consequences of any global warming that might occur. The latter effect will probably be minor compared with the former, at least for the next several decades. Thus, the precautionary principle argues against accelerating GHG reductions for the next few decades beyond what would occur due to secular improvements in technology (i.e., normal measures to reduce air pollution and energy-related costs) and removal of unjustified subsidies for energy and land use.

This argument is strengthened by the immediacy criterion because the problems due to forcing the pace of GHG reductions are likely to occur sooner than the negative effects of deferring such reductions. The argument is further bolstered by the uncertainty criterion because the negative effects of greater poverty are more certain than the positive effects of reducing climate change.

With respect to environmental consequences, the threats to habitat, carbon stores and sinks, and biodiversity arising from added GHG controls ought, over the next several decades, to outweigh the potential negative impacts of global warming. Moreover, any reduction in economic growth would make it that much harder to cope with adversities in general, whether they are connected to global warming or not.

There is no guarantee that forcing the pace of GHG controls will provide net global benefits for public health or, separately, for the environment, but there is a good likelihood that it may well worsen both. One could argue, therefore, that the precautionary principle requires that GHG reductions not be accelerated.

But there are counterarguments against deferring requirements to reduce GHG emissions.

First, given that the impacts of climate change could add to other environmental stresses on natural and human systems, climate change may be the straw that breaks the camel's back. Consider malaria, for instance: Because of climate change, malaria incidence in 2100 may climb from 500 million to between 550 and 580 million (Table 4-1).

But there are at least two ways to address the problem of the "last straw" (Goklany 1999d). The usual approach is to try to eliminate it. That means trying to forestall climate change completely in order to wipe out the 50 million to 80 million additional malaria cases projected for 2100. But we know that there will be some climate change even if atmospheric GHG concentrations can be stabilized immediately (which is most unlikely).

Alternatively, we could lighten the overall burden on the camel's back by removing several other straws to make room for that possible last straw. That would also leave a margin for error. Accordingly, we could focus on reducing the total 550 million to 580 million malaria cases that may occur in 2100 rather than concentrate only on the extra 50 million to 80 million. If the baseline rate of 500 million is reduced by just 0.2 percent per year from now to 2100, that would more than compensate for any increase in malaria attributable to climate change. And a 0.02 percent per year reduction would exceed any improvements that might result from the Kyoto Protocol.

Considering that a million Africans die from malaria annually and that it costs $8 to save a life-year from malaria (McNeil 2000), humanity would be better served if a billion dollars were spent now to reduce malaria (and other potentially climate-sensitive diseases) in the immediate future rather than spending tens, if not hundreds, of billions to limit climate change that may or may not reduce the burden of disease decades from now. Moreover, the knowledge gained from escalating anti-malaria efforts now will stand humanity in good stead if and when climate change increases the incidence of malaria. Such a strategy would provide more bang for the buck, and benefits to humanity would come sooner and more certainly. In effect, the first counterargument against deferring requirements for GHG controls is nullified by the adaptation and uncertainty criteria.

A second counterargument is that the assessment that the impacts of climate change will likely be small relative to other public health and environmental problems facing the globe is based on net global impacts. That assessment ignores the fact that there will be regional winners and losers because of the nonuniform geographical impacts of warming. In particular, developing countries may be the biggest losers because, being poor, they are the least able to adapt.

Consider food security, for example. Developing nations already run food deficits. Their net imports of grain currently amount to about 10 percent of their production (FAO 2001). Those deficits will get worse in the future because the increase in the demand for food in developing counties is expected to outstrip the increase in agricultural productivity (Goklany 1999d, Pinstrup-Andersen et al. 1999). Global warming is expected to further aggravate developing nations' food deficits even though developed countries' surpluses are expected to increase.

It is not necessary to require GHG reductions to address this issue, however. The potential increase in food deficits attributable to climate change can be addressed in exactly the same way as we address current imbalances in production (and differences in "comparative advantage") today—namely, through trade. Trade allows surpluses to flow voluntarily to deficit areas (Goklany 1995a, 1998a). But to expand such trade, developing countries will need to grow the non-food sectors of their economies (Goklany 2000a). And, as noted previously, economic growth has other ancillary benefits for human well-being. Thus, the second counterargument against aggressively forcing the pace of GHG controls is also invalidated by the adaptation criterion.

A third counterargument is that although climate change may not be the most urgent problem facing the globe over the next several decades, because of the inertia of the climate system it may be too late to do anything about warming by the time its impacts become urgent. In other words, climate change may not be as urgent as other environmental problems today and tomorrow, but it could be crucial the day after tomorrow. Table 4-1, however, suggests that even if there is a 50-year lead time to implement climate change controls, we have two or three decades of leeway before commencing any costly control actions (Wigley 1997, Wigley et al. 1996, Ha-Doung et al. 1997). Moreover, as Table 4-1 indicates, even if we could solve the problem of climate change, most of the critical underlying problems that placed climate change on the global policy agenda in the first place would still need to be addressed (Goklany 1992, 2000a). So one might win the battle over climate change, yet lose the war for the planet's—humanity's and the rest of nature's—well-being.

Consider forest and habitat losses. If human effect on climate change were completely halted (an unlikely proposition), we could still lose 25 percent of global forest area because the increasing future human demand for food could increase pressures to convert additional habitat for agriculture (see Table 4-1) (Goklany 2000a). Arbitrarily discounting (for the moment) the notion that climate change could increase global forest cover, as suggested by the IPCC (1996c; see Table 4-1), eliminating climate change would do little or nothing to reduce the major, imminent threats to global forests, ecosystems, biodiversity, and loss of carbon sinks and stores. Similarly, if human-induced climate change is eliminated, the challenge of adequately feeding the world's future population will be practically undiminished.

So how do we solve the urgent problems of today and tomorrow without compromising our ability to address the climate change problems of the day after?

There are two complementary approaches to addressing these multiple problems. First, we can focus on fixing those current and urgent environmental problems that might be aggravated by climate change (Goklany 1992, 1995a, 2000a). With respect to the problem of increasing forest and habitat loss, for instance, this means addressing its basic causes—the increased demand for land and water to meet human needs for food, clothing, shelter, paper, and other material goods. To reduce such demand, we should attempt to produce as much food, timber, and other products per unit of land and water as possible in an environmentally sound manner. That would also help solve the problem of food security because it would increase food production and help keep food prices in check. In addition, reductions in land conversion to agriculture would help maintain global carbon stocks and sinks, thereby mitigating carbon emissions. And by containing land costs, it would reduce costs for carbon sequestration or "energy" farms (to produce fuel wood for energy), if they are ever needed (Goklany 1998a, 1999c).

To increase the productivity and efficiency of land and water use, we ought to continue research and development on precision farming, integrated pest management, and methods to reduce postharvest and end-use crop and timber losses. Greater emphasis should also be placed on research and development to increase agricultural and forest productivity under less-than-optimal conditions, which might become more prevalent as a result of climate change. Such conditions include drought (caused by higher temperatures and re-distribution of precipitation), higher salinity (caused by greater evaporation and saltwater intrusion in coastal agricultural areas), and higher levels of carbon dioxide. Biotechnology, unless banned or greatly constrained, can play a crucial role in those endeavors (see Chapter 3). Genetically modified crops could also limit environmental damage associated with agriculture by reducing reliance on synthetic fertilizers and pesticides that eventually pollute both soil and water, and by increasing no-till cultivation, which, in turn, would further reduce soil erosion and water pollution. Lower levels of soil erosion and fertilizer use would also reduce GHG emissions—specifically, CO_2 and nitrous oxide. Pound-for-pound, nitrous oxide is over 300 times more powerful a GHG than CO_2 (see Chapter 3).

The second approach to addressing today's problems as well as tomorrow's is to reduce the vulnerability of society in general by increasing its resilience under adversity, whatever the cause (Goklany 1992, 1995a, 2000a). That can be accomplished by enhancing the mutually reinforcing forces of technological change, economic growth, and trade. As Figures 2-1, 2-2, and 4-4 through 4-7 illustrate, virtually every indicator of human or environmental well-being improves with wealth. Poorer countries are hungrier and have lower access to proper nutrition, medicines, public health technologies, safe water, and sanitation; consequently, their inhabitants suffer from poorer health, higher mortality rates, and live shorter lives. The fact that they have fewer resources (fiscal as well as human capital) to create, acquire, and operate new and existing-but-underutilized technologies makes them less resilient and more vulnerable to adversity.

Poverty makes nations more vulnerable not only to problems of public health but also to environmental problems. It has already been noted that poorer nations have lower access to safe water and sanitation (see Figure 4-6). They also use land less efficiently (see Figure 4-7), which translates into higher levels of habitat loss per unit of food produced and increased threats to biological diversity. As for air quality and other, less critical environmental indicators, as I have argued elsewhere, richer is cleaner and anything that retards economic growth eventually retards environmental improvements (Goklany 1995b, 1999b).

In essence, just as someone suffering from AIDS is less immune to infectious disease, no matter what the infection, so is a poorer society less immune to adversity, no matter what its proximate cause. And just as the drug AZT boosts the entire immune system of a person with AIDS, helping that person combat infection, economic growth boosts the ability of society to combat any adversity, and not just the adverse impacts of climate change (Goklany 1999d).

Economic growth enhances technological change, making society more resilient. In turn, technological change reinforces economic growth. Trade is also an integral part of boosting society's resilience. Not only does trade enable food and other natural resources to move voluntarily from surplus to deficit areas—in so doing it also discourages exploitation of marginal resources. It also helps disseminate new technologies and bolster economic growth (Goklany 1995a, 1995b).

To summarize, a comprehensive application of the precautionary principle points to caution over the next few decades in reducing GHG emissions. A more aggressive strategy could retard increases in global wealth, which could lead to greater hunger, poorer health, and higher mortality, as well as retard progress toward environmental improvements such as safer water, better sanitation, reduced habitat loss, and lowered threats to biodiversity. Specifically, the precautionary principle argues against forcing the pace of GHG controls beyond what would occur with secular improvements in technology. The principle argues instead for putting greater emphasis on research into the consequences of climate change, on solving current problems that may be worsened by climate change, and on enhancing society's adaptability and reducing its vulnerability to environmental problems by strengthening the institutions underpinning the mutually reinforcing forces of technological change, economic growth, and trade. These institutions, which co-evolve, include free markets, secure property rights, honest government, and predictable public policies.

Enhancing adaptability and reducing vulnerability will also raise the thresholds at which GHG concentrations become more "dangerous." That would be quite consistent with the United Nations Framework Convention on Climate Change's "ultimate objective," which, according to its Article 2, is to prevent anthropogenic climate change from becoming "dangerous," however that term may be defined (UNFCCC 1992, Goklany 2000a). And, in turn, that would reduce the social and economic costs of GHG controls.

Conclusion

The precautionary principle has been invoked to justify a policy of aggressive GHG emission controls. But that justification is based on a selective application of the precautionary principle. It takes credit for the potential adverse impacts of climate change that it would reduce but ignores any adverse consequences that it might generate or perpetuate. The justification also overlooks any potential positive effects of climate change that might have to be forgone.

Crash efforts to slow the increase in GHG atmospheric concentrations significantly in the short- to medium-term could, in the final analysis, decrease overall access to food and delay improvements in public health by slowing economic growth or increasing energy prices, or both. Poorer segments of society, especially in the developing world, would be most adversely affected. Contrary to claims that such a policy would be precautionary, it would in fact increase overall risks to public health and the environment. Thus, aggressive control policies (such as the Kyoto Protocol) might—perversely—throw the world, particularly the developing world, from the frying pan into the fire. This would be particularly ironic in view of the fact that one of the arguments for taking aggressive steps to reduce climate change now is that its impacts would be worse for developing countries because they cannot easily afford adaptive measures and technologies.

The precautionary principle properly applied, with full consideration of all the public health and environmental consequences of action and inaction, argues for substantially different policies:

- The precautionary principle argues against GHG emission reduction requirements in the next few decades if they go beyond secular improvements in technology and elimination of unjustified energy subsidies. Aggressive GHG controls are likely to retard economic development worldwide, which would lead to greater hunger, poorer health, and higher mortality, especially in developing countries.
- The precautionary principle argues against raising oil and gas prices because that would reduce the availability of food as well as slow down the abandonment of solid fuels for heating and cooking in the developing world, thus delaying reductions in mortality from indoor air pollution. Such requirements could

also reduce crop yields and increase land conversion, habitat loss, and threats to biodiversity.

- The precautionary principle argues for directly solving current urgent problems that may be aggravated by climate change. If we are truly concerned about malaria or malnutrition, we should expend our scarce resources (human and capital) to address these problems today. Such action would produce substantial benefits now, rather than several decades from now. On the other hand, reducing GHGs today, if it does any good at all, will not produce significant benefits for several decades.

- The precautionary principle argues for directly solving current urgent problems that would simultaneously reduce GHG concentrations in the atmosphere. That includes reducing unnecessary subsidies for energy and other natural resources, which only encourage overexploitation of marginal resources. Similarly, increasing agricultural productivity would increase food production and reduce hunger while reducing habitat conversion, soil erosion, and any associated loss of carbon stores and sinks.

- The precautionary principle argues for increasing society's adaptability and decreasing its vulnerability to environmental problems in general and climate change in particular. These objectives could be achieved by bolstering the institutions that are the foundations of the mutually reinforcing forces of technological change, economic growth, and trade. Such institutions include free markets, secure property rights, honest bureaucracies and governments, and predictable public policies. Moreover, consistent with the precautionary principle and the UNFCCC's "ultimate objective," enhancing adaptability and reducing vulnerability will raise the thresholds at which GHG concentrations become "dangerous." These efforts would also reduce the overall cost of whatever controls may be ultimately necessary.

- The precautionary principle argues for continued research and development into the science, impacts, economics, and policy analysis of climate change, as well as continued monitoring of climate change and its impacts so as to forestall nasty surprises in case the rates accelerate or the impacts come sooner or are worse than anticipated.

87

- The precautionary principle argues for continued research and development into alternative energy sources, and other methods of limiting the buildup of GHG concentrations in the atmosphere—including, as insurance, exotic approaches such as iron fertilization of oceans, just in case a quick fix becomes necessary.

Finally, some also view aggressive reductions in GHG emissions today as a form of insurance. But, as shown above, the world cannot afford the premium for such a policy. It would make little sense for a family to purchase an insurance policy with a premium large enough to jeopardize the breadwinner's ability to gas up the car to go to the job needed to keep the family clothed, fed, and sheltered. On the other hand, the truly precautionary policies suggested here would help humanity continue to progress while limiting its demands on the rest of nature.

5. Ensuring that Good Intentions Do Not Spawn Bad Outcomes

The precautionary principle has often been used as a rationale for policies that would severely restrict, if not ban, a variety of technologies. This book examines the public health and environmental consequences of three such policies: a global ban on DDT; a global ban on research, development, and commercialization of genetically modified crops; and forcing the pace of greenhouse gas controls beyond "no-regrets" actions, which conventional environmental wisdom has advanced as "precautionary." But there are dilemmas associated with these policies: Along with the benefits each might generate, each might also bring harm to public health and/or the environment. Unfortunately, the precautionary principle generally provides no guidance to resolve such dilemmas. Accordingly, I have proposed a framework that would allow the precautionary principle to be applied in situations in which the overall outcome might be ambiguous because the benefits of a policy might be overwhelmed by its harm.

This framework consists of a set of hierarchical criteria that can be used to rank the various threats that are increased or reduced by the policy under consideration based on the nature, magnitude, immediacy, uncertainty, and persistence of each threat, and the extent to which it can be alleviated. In this framework, threats to human health take precedence over threats to the environment.

The *public health criterion* can be decomposed into two component criteria. Foremost is the *human mortality criterion*, which specifies that the death of a human being takes precedence over the death of a member of another species. In addition, nonmortal threats to human health should outweigh threats to the environment, although there might be exceptions based on the nature, severity, and extent of the competing threats. This is the *human morbidity criterion*.

Application of this framework indicates, for example, that a global ban on DDT would increase public health risks in countries where malaria is still endemic. In 1999, 300 million cases and 1.1 million deaths were attributed to malaria worldwide. Virtually all were in the developing world. History shows that eliminating indoor spraying of DDT in the poorer countries increases malaria incidence whether or not substitutes are theoretically available. The reason for this is DDT's low cost: In developing countries costs are a major determinant of whether—and the extent to which—public health interventions are employed. The poorer the country, the more likely it will eschew such interventions.

By contrast, the public health benefits of banning DDT are conjectural and, if they occur at all, substantially delayed in time. Thus, even if a ban causes only a small increase in malaria cases, the increased risk to public health of discontinuing DDT use indoors will far exceed in magnitude, certainty, and immediacy any public health impacts of continuing its use. Therefore, indoor spraying should continue in countries where malaria is prevalent and where DDT use is effective, until equally safe and cost-effective substitutes become widely available and have been accepted voluntarily in those countries.

Given malaria's—and DDT's—significance for public health in the developing world, the development of DDT resistance in mosquitoes should be forestalled for as long as possible. Accordingly, while indoor DDT spraying should continue in malaria-prone areas, its other uses, particularly agricultural uses, should be discontinued.

On the other hand, a DDT ban can be justified in developed countries. First, DDT is no longer critical for their public health. They have eliminated their malaria problem, and if it should ever recur, they can afford substitutes. Second, a reduction in their use of DDT would reduce associated environmental impacts as well as any of its marginal, albeit speculative, adverse health impacts. But, in fact, these developed countries have already discontinued use of DDT. In those countries DDT levels measured in human adipose tissue, fish, birds, and other wildlife species have declined substantially, and DDT's most visible (and feared) environmental effects are being, or have been, reversed. Thus, in terms of the public health and the environment of the developed countries, an international agreement to ban DDT is more symbolic than substantive.

Another example is genetically modified crops. The application of the proposed framework shows that a ban on GM crops would retard reductions in global hunger, malnutrition, and diseases of affluence. Currently, more than 800 million people worldwide suffer from hunger and undernourishment, and more than 2 billion suffer from malnutrition. As a result, each year hunger and malnutrition kill more than 6 million children under the age of 5 years worldwide, and diseases of affluence kill almost 20 million. But relative to conventional crops, GM crops would increase the quantity and nutritional quality of food supplies, which should reduce mortality and morbidity rates worldwide. In contrast, the health effects of ingesting GM crops are uncertain, at best. So the effect of a GM crop ban is likely to be increased harm to public health.

By increasing productivity and reducing chemical inputs, GM crops would increase the amount of land and water available for the rest of nature and reduce the global pollution caused by fertilizers, pesticides, and carbon. The result would be greater protection of habitat, biological diversity, water quality, and the current climate than with conventional agriculture. Thus, contrary to conventional environmental wisdom, the precautionary principle, properly applied—with a more comprehensive consideration of the public health and environmental consequences of a ban—argues for a sustained effort to research, develop, and commercialize GM crops, provided reasonable caution is exercised.

Corollaries to this conclusion are that a GM ban would be directly counter to the raison d'être of the Convention on Biological Diversity and subsidiary agreements such as the Biosafety Protocol. If freedom from hunger and malnutrition is a basic human right, then the rights of hundreds of millions of people, who will continue to suffer from hunger and malnutrition (and any associated effects on health and welfare), will have been violated by a GM crop ban, which will effectively reduce the access to food and nutrition those millions would otherwise have had.

Use of the framework to evaluate a policy to force the pace of reductions in GHG emissions (beyond what might occur with secular improvements in technology and elimination of unjustified energy subsidies) indicates that such a policy would, more likely than not, increase overall risks to public health and the environment for the next several decades. Aggressive pursuit of GHG emission reductions beyond "no-regrets" actions would impede economic development, which would slow progress on combating hunger, improving health, and lowering mortality rates, especially in developing countries. Higher energy prices would reduce the availability of food because fossil fuels are a key input for the food and agricultural sector. It would also retard the replacement of solid fuels (e.g., coal, dung, and wood) with more environmentally benign fuels (e.g., oil, propane, and natural gas) for heating and cooking in the households of developing nations. According to the World Health Organization, the indoor air pollution in those nations caused by current heating and cooking practices is responsible for 2.8 million deaths annually.

Moreover, the same factors—lower levels of economic development and higher energy prices—would slow increases in crop yields, and this, in turn, would increase losses of habitat to cropland and increase threats to biological diversity. Therefore, there is no guarantee that aggressive GHG controls will not also be worse for the environment.

A policy to reduce vulnerability and increase adaptability to adversity in general, and climate change in particular, would—unlike a policy of aggressive GHG reductions—be consistent with the precautionary principle. Broad strategies in consonance with such a policy include, first, focusing on solving existing problems that may be exacerbated by climate change. Such problems include malaria, hunger, malnourishment, loss of habitat, and threats to biodiversity.

Another strategy would be to solve current urgent problems that would also limit GHG concentrations in the atmosphere. Measures consistent with this strategy include efforts to reduce deforestation and soil erosion and to limit subsidies that result in the overuse of energy and land.

A third strategy would be to ensure that societies, particularly developing societies, possess the wherewithal to withstand, or cope with, adversity, regardless of whether it is caused by anthropogenic climate change or some other natural or manmade agency. What is required is economic growth to generate the funds and the human capital needed to acquire, implement, operate, and maintain technologies that would reduce vulnerability and increase adaptability. To achieve this, the institutions that undergird economic growth and technological change should be strengthened. Those institutions include free markets, freer trade, secure property rights, honest bureaucracies and governments, predictable public policies, as well as institutions to advance education and research and development and to disseminate technology.

By solving existing problems and reducing current vulnerabilities, those broad strategies would provide benefits sooner, and more certainly, than efforts to reduce GHG emissions. In addition, those benefits will accrue whether or not the climate is changed by manmade GHG emissions or other (including natural) causes. Finally, enhancing adaptability and reducing vulnerability will raise the thresholds at which GHG concentrations become "dangerous," thereby reducing the overall cost of GHG controls. That would help postpone the imposition of GHG controls, which, in turn, would provide additional time for technological advances to reduce the cost (or enhance the cost-effectiveness) of controls.

Precautionary strategies for dealing with climate change should be supplemented by continuing research into the science, impacts, economics, and policy analysis of climate change. Such research should include monitoring of climate change and, more importantly, of its impacts, so as to obtain early warning of any nasty surprises should the rate of climate change accelerate or the impacts come sooner or be worse than anticipated. Research and development should also continue into alternative energy sources, and other methods of limiting GHG concentrations in the atmosphere—including, as insurance, exotic approaches such as iron fertilization of the oceans, just in case a rapid response becomes necessary.

Because of the large gaps between the harm generated by the three policies evaluated in this book and their benefits, the analyses using the proposed framework did not have to be very elaborate. But where there is a closer match between benefits and harms, the analysis of policies would probably have to be more quantitative, if not always more complex. Implementing the framework requires a heavy dose of scientific information regarding the magnitude, certainty, immediacy, persistence, and other characteristics of each of the benefits and harms associated with the policies. In addition, as the case studies indicate, analyses must consider the policies that would be in place in the absence of the particular policies under evaluation.

There is no shortage of other ambiguous policies that could be evaluated by using the framework. Such policies include:

- Additional control of sulfates and soot, which could improve public health and enhance visibility but also add to global warming;

- Incentives to construct or prolong the life span of nuclear power plants, which could reduce air pollution and global warming while raising the risk of nuclear radiation;
- Licensing of hydroelectric power plants, which could limit air pollution and global warming while affecting the quantity and timing of water available for in-stream uses;
- Allowing geoengineering options (e.g., iron fertilization of low-productivity ocean bodies) to reduce atmospheric concentration of carbon dioxide;
- Commercialization of specific GM crops or, for that matter, any particular agricultural technology—GM, organic, or conventional. Ideally, each of these policies should be evaluated on a case-by-case basis.

In summary, the precautionary principle has been touted as an approach to minimize, if not avoid, the unintended consequences of technology in general. But, as the three policies examined in this book amply demonstrate, the principle itself is not exempt from the law of unintended consequences.

Those policies, advanced as precautionary in order to protect the environment, provide vindication for the proposition that the road to hell is paved with good intentions. The wide gap between outcomes and intentions results from the fact that policies favored by conventional environmental wisdom are credited with the public health and environmental risks they might end, reduce, or forestall but are not debited with the risks they might create, increase, or prolong. Just as fiscal honesty demands an accountant to record fiscal debits as well as credits, intellectual honesty demands that evaluation of environmental policies consider both sides of the risk ledger. The framework offered here provides a mechanism for doing exactly that.

References

Adler, Jonathan H. 2000. More Sorry than Safe: Assessing the Precautionary Principle and the Proposed International Biosafety Protocol. *Texas International Law Journal* 35, 194–204.

Adler, Jonathan, et al. 2000. *Greenhouse Policy Without Regrets.* Washington: Competitive Enterprise Institute.

Agbiotechnet. 1999. Hot Topic: *Bt* Plants: Resistance and Other Issues. July 1999. www.agbiotechnet.com/topics/hot.asp. Visited February 4, 2000.

Apse, M. P., G. S. Aharon, W. A. Snedden, and E. Blumwald. 1999. Salt Tolerance Conferred by Overexpression of a Vacuolar Na+/H+ Antiport in *Arabidopsis. Science* 285, 1256–58.

Attaran, Amir, Donald R. Roberts, Chris F.Curtis, and Wenceslaus L. Klima. 2000. Balancing Risks on the Backs of the Poor. *Nature Medicine* 6, 729–31.

Ausubel, J. H. 1998. Resources and Environment in the 21st Century: Seeing Past the Phantoms. *World Energy Council Journal,* July, pp. 8–16.

Barro, Robert J. 1997. *Determinants of Economic Growth: A Cross-Country Empirical Study.* Cambridge, Mass: MIT Press.

Bate, Roger. 2000. The Political Economy of DDT and Malaria Control. *Energy and Environment* 11, 6.

Bender, William H. 1994. An End Use Analysis of Global Food Requirements. *Food Policy* 19, 381–95.

Besser, R. E., et al. 1995. Prevention of Cholera Transmission: Rapid Evaluation of the Quality of Municipal Water in Trujillo, Peru. *Bol Oficina Sanit Panam* 119, no. 3, 189–94.

Bloom, Barry R. 1999. The Future of Public Health. *Nature* 402 (Supplement): C63–C64.

Bolin, F. 1999. Leveling Land Mines with Biotechnology. *Nature Biotechnology* 17, 732.

Bryan, J.H., D. H. Foley, and R. W. Sutherst. 1996. Malaria Transmission and Climate Change in Australia. *Medical Journal of Australia* 164, 345–47.

Buchanan, Robert. 1999. *Statement to the Senate Committee on Agriculture, Nutrition, and Forestry.* October 6, 1999. www.senate.gov/~agriculture/buc99106.htm. Visited January 11, 2000.

Carpenter, Janet E., and Leonard P. Gianessi. 2001. *Agricultural Biotechnology: Updated Benefit Estimate*s. Washington: National Center for Food and Agricultural Policy.

Carpenter, S., N. F. Caraco, D. L. Correll, R. W. Howarth, A. N. Sharpley, and V. H. Smith. 1998. Nonpoint Pollution of Surface Waters with Phosphorus and Nitrogen. *Issues in Ecology,* No. 3, Summer. esa.sdsc.edu/carpenter.htm. Visited February 10, 2000.

Centers for Disease Control and Prevention (CDC). 2000a. U.S. HIV and AIDS cases reported through June 2000. *HIV/AIDS Surveillance Report* 12, no. 1. www.cdc.gov/hiv/stats/hasr1201.htm. Visited February 21, 2001.

_____. 2000b. WONDER database, 2000. Available at wonder.cdc.gov.

CeresNet. 1999. *Environmental Benefits of Agricultural Biotechnology.* February 2.

www.ceresnet.org/Cnetart/990202_Environ_Benefits-AgBio.txt. Visited February 10, 2000.

Chamberlain, D., and C.N. Stewart. 1999. Transgene Escape and Transplastomics. *Nature Biotechnology* 17, 330–31.

Chassy, Bruce, and Lisa Sheppard. 1999. GMO Food Safety Risk Is Negligible. *ACES News*, University of Illinois. www.ag.uiuc.edu/news/articles/943382465.html. Visited December 10, 1999.

Christy, J. R., et al. 2001. Differential Trends in Tropical Sea Surface and Atmospheric Temperatures since 1979. *Geophysical Research Letters* 28, 183–86.

Coghlan, Andrew. 1999. On Your Markers. *New Scientist.* www.newscientis.com/nsplus/insight/gmworld/ gmfood/gmnews97.html. Visited November 20, 1999.

Comstock, Gary. 2000. *Vexing Nature?: On the Ethical Case against Agricultural Biotechnology.* Boston: Kluwer.

Convention on Biological Diversity. 2000. Cartagena Protocol on Biosafety to the Convention on Biological Diversity. www.biodiv.org/biosafe/Protocol/html/Biosafe-Prot.html. Visited March 3, 2001.

Conway, Gordon. 2000. Food for All in the Twenty-First Century. *Environment* 42, 9–18.

Conway, Gordon, and Gary Toenniesen. 1999. Feeding the World in the Twenty-First Century. *Nature* 402 (supplement): C55–C58.

Cook, R. James. 1999. *Toward Science-Based Risk Assessment for the Approval and Use of Plants in Agriculture and Other Environments.* CGIAR/NAS Biotechnology Conference, October 21–22, 1999. www.cgiar.org/biotechc/mccalla.htm. Visited November 11, 1999.

Council on Environmental Quality. 1992. *Environmental Quality.* Washington: Council on Environmental Quality.

_____. 1993. *Environmental Quality.* Washington: Council on Environmental Quality.

_____. 1999. *Environmental Quality Statistics.* Washington: Council on Environmental Quality. ceq.eh.doe.gov/nepa/reports/statistics/aquatic.html.

Crawley, M. J., S. L. Brown, R. S. Hails, D. D. Kohn, and M. Rees. 2001. Biotechnology: Transgenic Crops in Natural Habitats. *Nature* 409, 682–83.

Cropper, Maureen L., and Paul R. Portney. 1992. Discounting Human Lives. *Resources,* no. 108, (Summer): 1–4.

Cross, Frank B. 1996. Paradoxical Perils of the Precautionary Principle. *Washington and Lee Review* 53, no. 3, 851–925.

_____. 1998. *Could Kyoto Kill? The Mortality Costs of Climate Policies.* Washington: Competitive Enterprise Institute.

Daniell, Henry. 1999. The Next Generation of Genetically Engineered Crops for Herbicide and Insect Resistance: Containment of Gene Pollution and Resistant Insects. *AgBiotechNet,* Vol.1, August, ABN 024. www.agbiotechnet.com/reviews/aug99/html/Daniell.htm. Visited February 12, 2000.

Davies, C. R, et al. 1994. The Fall and Rise of Andean Cutaneous Leishmaniasis: Transient Impact of the DDT Campaign in Peru. *Transactions of the Royal Society for Tropical Medicine and Hygiene* 88, 389–93.

De la Fuente J. M., V. Ramírez-Rodríguez, J. L. Cabrera-Ponce, and L. Herrera-Estrella. 1997. Aluminum Tolerance in Transgenic Plants by Alteration of Citrate Synthesis. *Science* 276, 1566–68.

Dye, Chris, and Reiter, Paul. 2000. Climate Change and Malaria: Temperatures without Fevers. *Science* 289, 1697–98.

References

Easterlin, Richard A. 1996. *Growth Triumphant: The Twenty-First Century in Historical Perspective*. Ann Arbor: University of Michigan Press.

Edwards, G. 1999. Tuning Up Crop Photosynthesis. *Nature Biotechnology* 17, 22–23.

Encyclopedia Britannica. 1959. Chicago: William Benton.

Energy Information Administration. 1998. *What Does the Kyoto Protocol Mean to U.S. Energy Markets and the U.S. Economy?* SR/OIAF/98-03(S). Washington: Energy Information Administration.

Environmental Defense Fund. 1972. *Special Bulletin to EDF Members*. Newsletter, Vol. III, no. 3.

———. 1997. *25 Years after DDT Ban, Bald Eagles, Osprey Numbers Soar*. Press release. June 13, 1997. www.edf.org/pubs/NewsReleases/1997/Jun/e_ddt.html. Visited December 21, 1999.

Environmental Network News. 1998. Group Urges Global DDT Ban by 2007. July 1. Available at www.enn.com/enn-news-archive/1998/07/070198/ddt_22472.asp. Visited March 3, 2001.

Environmental Protection Agency. 2000a. Bt. *Corn Insect Resistance Management Announced for 2000 Growing Season*. EPA Headquarters Press Release. January 14, 2000.

———. 2000b. *October 18–20, 2000 FIFRA SAP Meeting: Bt Plant Pesticides Risk and Benefits Assessment*. Page 17. www.epa.gov/scipoly/sap/2000/october/questions.pdf. Visited March 3, 2001.

Fan, S., et al. 1998. A Large Terrestrial Carbon Sink in North America Implied by Atmospheric and Oceanic Carbon Dioxide Data and Models. *Science* 282, 442–46.

Ferber, Dan. 1999. Risks and Benefits: GM Crops in the Cross Hairs. *Science* 286, 1662–66.

Ferber, Dan. 2000. Superbugs on the Hoof. *Science* 288, 792–94.

Food and Agricultural Organization. 1997. *The State of the World's Forests 1997*. Rome: Food and Agricultural Organization.

———. 1999a. *FAOSTAT Database*. www.apps.fao.org. Visited January 12, 2000.

———. 1999b. The State of Food Insecurity in the World. FAO Rome. www.fao.org/FOCUS/E/SOFI/home-e.htm. Visited January 12, 2000.

———. 2000. *FAOSTAT Database*. www.apps.fao.org. Visited December 12, 2000.

———. 2001. *FAOSTAT Database*. www.apps.fao.org. Visited March 3, 2001.

Food and Agricultural Organization/World Health Organization. 1996. *Biotechnology and Food Safety. Report of a Joint FAO/WHO Consultation*. Rome, Italy, September 30 to October 4. www.fao.org/waicent/faoinfo/economic/esn/biotech/six.htm. June 12, 2000.

Frederick, Kenneth M., Indur M. Goklany, and Norman J. Rosenberg. 1994. Conclusions, Remaining Issues, and Next Steps. *Climatic Change* 28, 209–19.

French, C. F., S. J. Rosser, G. J. Davies, S. Nicklin, and N. C. Bruce. 1999. Biodegradation of Explosives by Transgenic Plants Expressing Pentaerythritol Tetranitrate Reductase. *Nature Biotechnology* 17, 491–94.

Friends of the Earth. 1999a. *FoE Supports Tory GM Moratorium Call. What about the Precautionary Principle, Mr. Blair*. www.foe.co.uk/pubsinfo/infoteam/press-rel/1999/19990203170456.html. Visited May 15, 2000.

———. 1999b. *FoE Remains Sceptical about Monsanto's Terminator Pledge*. Press Release, October 5. www.foeeurope.org/press/foe_remains_sceptical.htm. Visited February 21, 2000.

Frommer, Wolf B., Uwe Ludewig, and Doris Rentsch. 1999. Taking Transgenic Plants with a Pinch of Salt. *Science* 285, 1222–23.

Gaffen, D. J., and R. J. Ross. 1998. Increased Summertime Heat Stress in the U.S. *Nature* 396, 529–30.

Gendel, S. 1999. *The Biotechnology Information for Food Safety Database.* www.iit.edu/ ~sgendel/fa.htm. Visited January 11, 2000.

Glowka, L., F. Burhenne-Guilmin, and H. Synge. 1994. *A Guide to the Convention on Biological Diversity.* Gland, Switzerland: World Conservation Union (IUCN).

Goklany, Indur M. 1992. *Adaptation and Climate Change.* Paper presented at the Annual Meeting of the American Association for the Advancement of Science, Chicago, February 6–11, 1992. Available from the author.

_____. 1994. *Air and Inland Surface Water Quality: Long Term Trends and Relationship to Affluence.* Washington: Office of Program Analysis, U.S. Department of the Interior.

_____. 1995a. Strategies to Enhance Adaptability: Technological Change, Economic Growth and Free Trade. *Climatic Change* 30, 427–49.

_____. 1995b. Richer Is Cleaner: Long Term Trends in Global Air Quality. In *The True State of the Planet.* Edited by Ronald Bailey. New York: Free Press, pp. 339–77.

_____. 1996. Factors Affecting Environmental Impacts: The Effects of Technology on Long Term Trends in Cropland, Air Pollution and Water-Related Diseases. *Ambio* 25, 497–503.

_____. 1998a. Saving Habitat and Conserving Biodiversity on a Crowded Planet. *BioScience* 48, 941–53.

_____. 1998b. The Importance of Climate Change Compared to Other Global Changes. In: *Proceedings of the Second International Specialty Conference on Global Climate Change: Science, Policy, and Mitigation/Adaptation Strategies, Crystal City, Va., October 13–16, 1998.* Sewickley, Penn.: Air & Waste Management Association, 1024–41.

_____. 1999a. *The Future of Industrial Society.* Paper presented at the International Conference on Industrial Ecology and Sustainability, University of Technology of Troyes, Troyes, France, September 22–25.

_____. 1999b. *Clearing the Air: The True Story of the War on Air Pollution.* Washington: Cato Institute.

_____. 1999c. Meeting Global Food Needs: The Environmental Trade-Offs between Increasing Land Conversion and Land Productivity. *Technology* 6, 107–30.

_____. 1999d. Richer Is More Resilient: Dealing with Climate Change and More Urgent Environmental Problems. In *Earth Report 2000, Revisiting the True State of the Planet.* Edited by R. Bailey. New York: McGraw-Hill, pp. 155–87.

_____. 2000a. Potential Consequences of Increasing Atmospheric CO_2 Concentration Compared to Other Environmental Problems. *Technology* 7S, 189–213.

_____. 2000b. *Applying the Precautionary Principle to Global Warming.* St. Louis: Center for the Study of American Business, Washington University. Policy Study 158.

_____. 2000c. Applying the Precautionary Principle in a Broader Context. In *Rethinking Risk and the Precautionary Principle.* Edited by Julian Morris. Oxford: Butterworth-Heinemann, pp. 189–228.

_____. 2000d. *Applying the Precautionary Principle to Genetically Modified Crops.* St. Louis: Center for the Study of American Business, Washington University. Policy Study 157.

_____. 2001a. *Economic Growth and the State of Humanity.* Bozeman, Mont.: Political Economy Research Center. Policy Series 21.

_____. 2001b. Precaution without Perversity: A Comprehensive Application of the Precautionary Principle to Genetically Modified Crops. *Biotechnology Law Report* 20, no. 3, 377–96.

Goklany, Indur M., and Merritt W. Sprague. 1991. *An Alternative Approach to Sustainable Development: Conserving Forests, Habitat and Biological Diversity by Increasing the Efficiency and Productivity of Land Utilization.* Washington: Office of Program Analysis, Department of the Interior.

Goklany, Indur M., and Soren R. Straja. 2000. U.S. Death Rates Due to Extreme Heat and Cold Ascribed to Weather, 1979–1997. *Technology 7S,* 165–73.

Goklany, Indur M., Roger Bate, and Kendra Okonski. 2001. Will Children Eat GM Rice, or Risk Blindness from Vitamin A Deficiency? *British Medical Journal.* Online. Letter. Available at: www.bmj.com/cgi/eletters/322/7279/126/b#EL1. Visited February 9, 2001.

Goldstein, Larry J., David C. Lay, and David I. Schneider. 1999. *Calculus and Its Applications.* 4th Ed. Upper Saddle River, N.J.: Prentice Hall.

Goto, F., et al. 1999. Iron Fortification of Rice Seed by the Soybean Ferritin Gene. *Nature Biotechnology* 17, 282–86.

Gould, Fred. 1998. Sustaining the Efficacy of *Bt* Toxins. In *Agricultural Biotechnology and Environmental Quality: Gene Escape and Pest Resistance.* Edited by R. W. F. Hardy and J. B. Segelken. Ithaca, N.Y.: National Agricultural Biotechnology Council. Report 10, pp. 77–86.

Grabau Laboratory. 1998. *Improving Phosphorus Utilization in Soybean Meal through Phytase Gene Engineering.* February 19. www.biotech.vt.edu/plants/grabau/projects.html. Visited February 9, 2000.

Gray, A. 1998. Nature Debates: Be Careful What You Wish. . .. 15 October. www.biotech-info.net/monarch_Q&A.html. Visited February 12, 2000.

Gray, A. J., and A. F. Raybould. 1998. Reducing Transgene Escape Routes. *Nature* 392, 653–54.

Greenpeace. 1998. *Stop Monsanto's Terminator Technology.* www.greenpeace.org~geneng/highlights/pat/98_09_20.htm. Visited January 12, 2000.

Grieco, John P., Nicole L. Achee, Richard G. Andre, and Donald R. Roberts. 2000. A Comparison Study of House Entering Behavior of *Anopheles vestitipennis (Diptera: Culicidae)* Using Experimental Huts Sprayed with DDT or Deltamethrin in the Southern District of Toledo, Belize, C.A. *Journal of Vector Ecology* 25, no. 1, 62–73.

Guarda, Javier A., Cesar Ramal Asayag, and Richard Witzig. 1999. Malaria Reemergence in the Peruvian Amazon Region. *Emerging Infectious Diseases* 5, 209–15.

Guardian. 2000. Malaria Impedes Development in Africa. May 12, 2000. Available at www.newafrica.com/newsarchivesq220000/may/socialnews.asp. Visited October 2, 2000.

Guerinot, Mary Lou. 2000. The Green Revolution Strikes Gold. *Science* 287, 241–43.

Gura, Trisha. 1999. New Genes Boost Rice Nutrients. *Science* 285, 994–95.

Ha-Duong, M., M. J. Grubb, and J.-C. Hourcade. 1997. Influence of Socioeconomic Inertia and Uncertainty on Optimal (sic) CO_2-Emission Abatement. *Nature* 390, 270–73.

Harding, Keith. 1999. Biosafety of Selectable Marker Genes. BINAS On-line. United Nations Industrial Development Organization. www.bdt.org.br/binas/index.html. Visited June 12, 2000.

Harvard University Center for International Development and the London School of Hygiene and Tropical Medicine. 2000. Economics of Malaria. Executive Summary. www.malaria.org/jdsachseconomic.html. Visited October 2, 2000.

Hawksworth, D. L., et al. 1995. Magnitude and Distribution of Biodiversity. In *Global Bioiversity Assessment.* Edited by V. H. Heywood et al. Cambridge: Cambridge University Press, pp. 107–92.

Henderson-Sellers, Ann, et al. 1998. Tropical Cyclones and Global Climate Change: A Post-IPCC Assessment. *Bulletin of the American Meteorological Society* 79, 19–38.

Hilbeck, A., M. Baumgartner, P. M. Fried, and F. Bigler. 1998. Effects of Transgenic *Bacillus thuringiensis* Corn-Fed Prey on Mortality and Development Time of Immature *Chysoperla carnea (Neuroptera: Chrysopidae). Environmental Entomology* 27, no. 2, 480–87.

Hindu Business Line. 2000. Bt *Cotton Trials Show Yield Rise*. www.indiaserver.com/bline/2000/01/19/stories/071903a1.htm. Visited January 19, 2000.

Howard, L. O. 1909. Economic Loss to the People of the United States through Insects That Carry Disease. *National Geographic* 20, 735–49.

Huston, Michael A. 1994. *Biological Diversity*. Cambridge: Cambridge University Press, pp. 30–35.

Idso, C.D. and Idso, K. E. 2000. Forecasting World Food Supplies: The Impact of the Rising Atmospheric CO_2 Concentration. *Technology* 7S, 33–56.

Inside Purdue. 1998. *Raghothama: Phosphorus Uptake Gene Discovered*. www.purdue.edu/PER/ 1.13.98.IP.html. Visited January 19, 2000.

International Food Information Council. 1999. *Backgrounder—Food Biotechnology*. Updated April 1999. ificinfo.health.org/backgrnd/BKGR14.htm. Visited January 12, 2000.

Intergovernmental Panel on Climate Change. 1991. Resource Use and Management. In *Response Strategies: The Intergovernmental Panel on Climate Change*. Washington: Island Press, Chapter 6.

_____. 1996a. *Climate Change 1995: The Economic and Social Dimensions of Climate Change*. Cambridge: Cambridge University Press.

_____. 1996b. *Climate Change 1995: The Science of Climate Change*. Cambridge: Cambridge University Press.

_____. 1996c. *Climate Change 1995: Impacts, Adaptations and Mitigation of Climate Change*. Cambridge: Cambridge University Press.

_____. 2001a. Summary for Policymakers: IPCC WGI Third Assessment Report.

_____. 2001b. Summary for Policymakers: IPCC WGII Third Assessment Report.

International Rice Research Institute. 1999. Nitrogen-Fixing Rice Moves Closer to Reality. *IRRI Science Online*. December 21. www.iclarm.org/irri/Science.html. Visited February 1, 2000.

Jacobson, Mark Z. 2001. Strong Radiative Heating Due to Mixing State of Black Carbon in Atmospheric Aerosols. *Nature* 409, 695–97.

Jaglo-Ottosen, Kirsten et al. 1998. Arabidopsis CBF-1 Overexpression Induces COR Genes and Enhances Freezing Tolerance. *Science* 280, 104–106.

Jesse, L. C. H., and J. J. Obrycki. 2000. Field Deposition of *Bt* Transgenic Corn Pollen: Lethal Effects on the Monarch Butterfly. *Oecologia* 125, 241–48.

Johnson, B. 1999. Conserving Our Natural Environment. *Nature Biotechnology* 17, BV29–BV30.

Joint Program on the Science and Policy of Global Change. 2000. *Multi-Gas Strategies and the Cost of Kyoto*. Climate Policy Note 3.

Jordan, Andrew, and Timothy O'Riordan. 1999. The Precautionary Principle in Contemporary Environmental Policy and Politics. In *Protecting Public Health and the Environment: Implementing the Precautionary Principle*. Edited by Carolyn Raffensperger and Joel Tickner. Washington: Island Press, pp. 15–35.

Kasuga, M., Q. Liu, S. Miura, K. Yamaguchi-Shinozaki, and K. Shinozaki. 1999. Improving Plant Drought, Salt, and Freezing Tolerance by Gene Transfer of a Single Stress-Inducible Transcription Factor. *Nature Biotechnology* 17, 287–91.

Kathmandu Post. 2000. February 24. Consumption Pattern Found Shifting. www.nepalnews.com.np/ contents/englishdaily/ktmpost/2000/feb/feb24. Visited April 7, 2001.

Kershen, Drew L. 2001. The Risks of Going Non-GMO. *Oklahoma Law Review* 53, no. 4, forthcoming, footnote 46.

Kilbourne, E. M. 1997a. Cold Environments. In *The Public Health Consequences of Disasters*. Edited by E. K. Noji. New York: Oxford University Press, pp. 270–86.

_____. 1997b. Heat Waves and Hot Environments. In *The Public Health Consequences of Disasters*. Edited by E. K. Noji. New York: Oxford University Press, pp. 245–69.

Kota, M., H. Daniell, S. Varma, F. Garczynski, F. Gould, and W. J. Moar. 1999.Overexpression of the *Bacillus thuringiensis* (*Bt*) CRY2A2 Protein in Chloroplasts Confers Resistance to Plants against Susceptible and Bt-resistant Insects. *Proceedings of the National Academy of Sciences* 96, 1840–45.

Ku, M. S. B., et al. 1999. High-level Expression of Maize Phosphoenolpyruvate Carboxylase in Transgenic Plants. *Nature Biotechnology* 17, 76–80.

Lawrence, Eleanor. 1999. Biotechnology: Plastic Plants. *Nature Science Update.* September 28. helix.nature.com/nsu/990930-5.html. Visited January 11, 2000.

Lazaroff, Cat. 1999. Activists List Wins, Losses for 1900s. *Environmental News Service.* December 31. forests.org/archive/america/party99.htm. Visited April 14, 2001.

Leggett, Jeremy. 1990. Global Warming: A Greenpeace View. In *Global Warming: A Greenpeace Report*. Edited by Jeremy Leggett. Oxford: Oxford University Press, pp. 457–80.

Lemaux, Peggy G. 1999. *Plant Growth Regulators and Biotechnology.* Paper presented at the Western Plant Growth Regulator Society; January 13, Anaheim, Calif. plantbio.berkeley.edu/~outreach/ REGULATO.HTM. Visited January 19, 2000.

Lewis, R., and B. A. Palevitz. 1999. Science vs. P.R.: GM Crops Face Heat of Debate. *The Scientist*, Vol 13, October 11. www.the-scientist.library.upenn.edu/yr1999/oct/lewis_p1_991011.html. Visited January 19, 2000.

Liljegren, Sarah J., et al. 2000. *SHATTERPROOF* MADS-box Gene Control Seed Dispersal in *Arabidopsis*. *Nature* 404, 766–70.

Lindzen, Richard S., Ming-Dah Chou, and Arthur Y. Hou. Does the Earth Have an Adaptive Infrared Iris? *Bulletin of the American Meteorological Society* 82, 417–32.

Linnemann, H., J. De Hoogh, M. A. Keyzer, H. D. J. Van Heemst, R. J. Brolsma, J. N. Bruinsma, P. Buringh, G. J. Staring, and C. T. De Wit. 1979. *MOIRA: Model of International Relations in Agriculture*. Amsterdam: North Holland.

Liu Y.-B., B. E. Tabashnik, T. J. Dennehy, A. J. Patin, and A. C. Bartlett. 1999. Development Time and Resistance to *Bt* Crops. *Nature* 400, 519.

Losey, John E., Linda S. Rayor, and Maureen E. Carter. 1999. Transgenic Pollen Harms Monarch Larvae. *Nature* 399, 214.

MacIlwain, Colin. 1999. Access Issues May Determine Whether Agri-Biotech Will Help the World's Poor. *Nature* 402, 341–45.

Magnuson, John J., et al. 2000. Historical Trends in Lake and River Ice Cover in the Northern Hemisphere. *Science* 289, 1743–46.

Malakoff, D. 1997. Thirty Kyotos Needed to Control Warming. *Science* 278, 2048.

Mann, Charles C. 1999a. Crop Scientists Seek a New Revolution. *Science* 283, 310–14.

_____. 1999b. Genetic Engineers Aim to Soup Up Crop Photosynthesis. *Science* 283, 314–16.

_____. 1999c. Biotech Goes Wild. *Technology Review.* July/August.

Masood, E. 1997. Kyoto Agreement Creates New Agenda for Climate Research. *Nature* 390, 649–50.

May, Robert. 1999. *Genetically Modified Foods: Facts, Worries, Policies and Public Confidence*. Briefing from the Chief Science Officer, February. www.gn.apc.org/pmhp/dc/genetics/cso-gmos.htm. Visited February 21, 2000.

Mazur, Barbara, Enno Krebbers, and Scott Tingey. 1999. Gene Discovery and Product Development for Grain Quality Traits. *Science* 285, 372–75.

McMichael, A. J., et al.1996a. Human Population Health. In IPCC. 1996c. *Climate Change 1995: Impacts, Adaptations and Mitigation of Climate Change*. Cambridge: Cambridge University Press, pp. 561–84.

McMichael, A. J., et al., eds. 1996b. *Climate Change and Human Health*. Geneva: World Health Organization.

McNeil, Donald G., Jr., 2000. Selling Cheap Generic Drugs, India's Copycats Irk Industry. *The New York Times*, December 1, A1, A14.

Meade, Birgit, and Stacey Rosen. 1996. Income and Diet Differences Greatly Affect Food Spending Around the Globe. *Food Review*, September 1996. Washington: U.S. Department of Agriculture/Economic Research Service.

Meiners, Roger E., and Andrew P. Morriss. 2001. *Pesticides and Property Rights*. Bozeman, Mont: Political Economy Research Center. Policy Series 22.

Michaels, Patrick, and Robert Balling. 2000. *The Satanic Gases: Clearing the Air about Global Warming*. Washington: Cato Institute.

Michigan Technological University. 1999. *New Aspen Could Revolutionize Pulp and Paper Industry*. October 11. www.admin.mtu.edu/urel/breaking/1999/aspen.htm. Visited January 10, 2000.

Mikesell, L. 1999. Ag Biotech May Help Save the Bay. www.bio.org/food&ag/cbf.html. Visited February 21, 2000.

Milius, S. New Studies Clarify Monarch Worries. *Science News* 156, 391.

Moffat, Anne S. 1999a. Crop Engineering Goes South. *Science* 285, 370–71.

_____. 1999b. Engineering Plants to Cope with Metals. *Science* 285, 369–70.

Morris, Julian. 2000. In *Rethinking Risk and the Precautionary Principle*. Edited by Julian Morris. Oxford: Butterworth-Heinemann, pp. 1–21.

Morton, R. 2001. One More Reason Why *Bt* Crops More Safe than *Bt* Sprays. *Agbioview*: February 16. Archived at www.agbioview.org.

Munkvold, G. P., and R. L. Hellmich. 1999. Genetically Modified, Insect Resistant Corn: Implications for Disease Management. APSnet Plant Pathology Online, APSnet Feature, October 15 through November 30. www.scisoc.org/feature/BtCorn/Top.html. Visited February 19, 2000.

Myneni, R. B., et al. 1997. Increased Plant Growth in the Northern High Latitudes. *Nature* 386, 698–702.

Nakicenovic, N., A Grübler, and A. McDonald, eds. 1998. *Global Energy Perspectives*. Cambridge: Cambridge University Press.

National Academies News. 2001. Impact of Climate Change on Human Health Is "Highly Uncertain." News Release, April 2.

National Research Council. 1999. *Hormonally Active Agents in the Environment*. Washington: National Academy Press.

_____. 2001. *Under the Weather: Climate, Ecosystem, and Infectious Disease*. Washington: National Academy Press.

Nicholls, Neville. 1997. Increased Australian Wheat Yield Due to Recent Climate Trends. *Nature* 387, 484–85.

Oerke, E.-C., A. Weber, H.-W. Dehne, and F. Schonbeck. 1994. Conclusion and Perspectives. In *Crop Production and Crop Protection: Estimated Losses in Food and Cash*

Crops. Edited by E.-C. Oerke, A. Weber, H.-W. Dehne, and F. Schonbeck. Amsterdam: Elsevier, pp. 742–70.

Olsson, M., et al. Comparison of Temporal Trends (1940s–1990s) of DDT and PCB in Baltic Sediment and Biota in Relation to Sediment. *Ambio* 29, 195–201.

Pearce, D. W., et al. 1996. The Social Costs of Climate Change: Greenhouse Damage and the Benefits of Control. In IPCC. 1996a. *Climate Change 1995: Economic and Social Dimensions of Climate Change.* New York: Cambridge University Press, p. 191.

Pennisi, E. 1998. Plant biology: Transferred Gene Helps Plants Weather Cold Snaps. *Science* 280, 36.

Perry, John S. 1999. Climate Change—The Potential for Surprises. *Journal of the Federation of American Scientists* 52, no. 4. Available at www.fas.org/faspir/V52N4.htm.

Pesticide Action Network. Undated. DDT Fact Sheet. Available at www.pan-uk.org/actives/ddt.htm. Visited October 9, 2000.

Philander, S. George. *Is the Temperature Rising?: The Uncertain Science of Global Warming.* Princeton, N.J.: Princeton University Press.

Physicians for Social Responsibility. 1999. *Physicians Call for Complete Phase Out of DDT.* Press Release. August 30.

Pinheiro, F. P., and Chuit, R. 1998. Emergence of Dengue Hemorrhagic Fever in the Americas. *Infections in Medicine* 15, no. 4, 244–51.

Pinstrup-Andersen, P., R. Pandya-Lorch, and M.W. Rosegrant. 1999. *World Food Prospects: Critical Issues for the Twenty-First Century.* Washington: International Food Policy Research Institute.

Porter, R., ed. 1996. *The Cambridge Illustrated History of Medicine.* New York: Cambridge University Press.

Prakash, C. S. 1998a. Engineering Cold Tolerance Takes a Major Step Forward. *ISB News,* May. www.isb.vt.edu/news/1998/news98.may.html#may9802. Visited January 15, 2000.

———. 1998b. A First Step Towards Engineering Improved Phosphorus Uptake. *ISB News,* May. www.isb.vt.edu/news/1998/news98.may.html#may9802. Visited January 15, 2000.

———. 1999. *Relevance of Biotechnology to Indian Agriculture.* www.teriin.org/discuss/biotech/ abstracts.htm. Visited January 15, 2000.

Pritchett, Lant, and Lawrence H. Summers. 1996. Wealthier Is Healthier. *Journal of Human Resources* 31, 841–68.

Raffensperger, Carolyn, and Joel Tickner, eds. 1999. *Protecting Public Health and the Environment: Implementing the Precautionary Principle.* Washington: Island Press.

Raloff, Janet. 2000. The Case for DDT. *Science News* 158, 12–14.

Rayl, A. J. S. 2000. Are All Alien Invasions Bad? *The Scientist* 14 (March 20). www.the-scientist.com/yr2000/mar/rayl_p15_000320.html. Visited March 21, 2000.

Regal, Philip J. 1994. Scientific Principles for Ecologically Based Risk Assessment of Transgenic Organisms. *Molecular Ecology* 3:5–13. www.psrast.org/pjrisk.htm. Visited January 11, 2000.

Reilly, J., et al. 1996. Agriculture in a Changing Climate: Impacts and Adaptations. In IPCC. 1996c. *Climate Change 1995: Impacts, Adaptations and Mitigation of Climate Change.* Cambridge: Cambridge University Press, pp. 427–67.

Reiter, Paul. 1996. Global Warming and Mosquito-Borne disease in USA. *Lancet* 348, 622.

———. 2000. From Shakespeare to Defoe: Malaria in England in the Little Ice Age. *Emerging Infectious Diseases* 6, 1–11.

Richard, Cindy Lynn. *CBS News Covers Iowa Researcher's Study on* Bt *Corn Pollen and Monarch Butterfly Larvae.* Council for Agricultural Science and Technology. www.cast-science.org/biotechnology/ 20000821.htm. Visited February 13, 2001.

Roberts, D. R. 1999. Foreword: DDT Is Still Needed for Malaria Control. In *The Economic Costs of Malaria in South Africa: Malaria Control and the DDT Issue.* Edited by Richard Tren. www.iea.org.uk/env/malaria.htm. Visited December 12, 1999.

Roberts, D.R., et al. 1997. DDT, Global Strategies, and a Malaria Control Crisis in South America. *Emerging Infectious Diseases* 3, 295–301.

Roberts, D.R., S. Manguin, and J. Mouchet. 2000a. A Probability Model of Vector Behavior: Effects of DDT Repellency, Irritancy, and Toxicity in Malaria Control. *Journal of Vector Control* 25, no. 1, 48–61.

_____. 2000b. DDT House Spraying and Re-Emerging Malaria. *Lancet* 356, 330–32.

Rogers, David J., and Sarah E. Randolph. 2000. The Global Spread of Malaria in a Future, Warmer. *Science* 289, 1763–66.

Rosenberg, H. M., et al. 1996. Births and Deaths: United States, 1995. *Monthly Vital Statistics Report* 45, no. 3 (supp. 2), 31.

Rosenzweig, Cynthia, and Martin L. Parry. 1994. Potential Impacts of Climate Change on World Food Supply. *Nature* 367, 133–38.

Royal Society. 1998. *Genetically Modified Plants for Food Use.* www.royalsoc.ac.uk/st_pol40.htm Visited January 11, 2000.

Sagoff, Mark. 1999. What's Wrong with Exotic Species? *Report from the Institute for Philosophy and Public Policy* 19 (Fall): 16–23.

Saxena, D., S. Flores, and G. Stotzky. 1999. Transgenic Plants: Insecticidal Toxin in Root Exudates from *Bt* Corn. *Nature* 402, 480.

Saxena, D., and G. Stotzky. 2001. *Bt* Toxin Uptake from Soil by Plants. *Nature Biotechnology* 19, 199.

Scalise, Kathleen. 1997. *New Solution for Food Allergies Effective with Milk, Wheat Products, Maybe Other Foods, UC Researchers Discover.* University of California, Berkeley News Release. October 19. www.urel.berkeley.edu/urel_1/CampusNews/Press Releases/releases/10_19_97a.html. Visited January 5, 2000.

Schmitt, C. J., J. L. Zajicek, and P. H. Peterman. 1990. National Pesticide Monitoring Program. *Archives of Environmental Contamination and Toxicology* 19, 748–81.

Science. 2000. Corrections and Clarifications. *Science* 288, 1751.

Scott, S. E., and M. J. Wilkinson. 1999. Low Probability of Chloroplast Movement from Oilseed Rape (*Brassica rapus*) into Wild *Brassica rapa. Nature Biotechnology* 17, 390–92.

Severo, O. P. 1955. Eradication of the Aedes aegypti Mosquito from the Americas. In *Yellow Fever. A Symposium in Commemoration of Carlos Juan Finlay. The Jefferson Medical College of Philadelphia, 22–23 September 1955,* 39–59.

Sharma, V. P. 1996. Re-Emergence of Malaria in India. *Indian Journal of Medical Research* 103, 26–45.

Sheridan, Mary Beth. 2000. A Delicate Balancing Act in Mexico. *Los Angeles Times,* February 29.

Shiklomanov, Igor A. 2000. Appraisal and Assessment of World Water Resources. *Water International* 25, no. 1: 11–32.

Simon, Julian L. 2000. More People, Greater Wealth, Abundant Resources, Cleaner Environment. In *Population: The Ultimate Resource.* Edited by Barun Mitra. New Delhi: Liberty Institute, pp. 1–18.

Singer, S. Fred. 1997. Hot Talk, Cold Science: Global Warning's Unfinished Debate. Oakland, Calif.: Independent Institute.

References

Skei, J., et al. 2000. Eutrophication and Contaminants in Aquatic Ecosystems. *Ambio* 29, 184–94.

Sleigh, A. C., Xi-Li Liu, S. Jackson, Peng Li, and Le-Yuan Shang. 1998. Resurgence of Vivax Malaria in Henan Province, China. *Bulletin of the World Health Organization* 76:

Smaglik, Paul. 1998. Success of Edible Vaccine May Depend on Picking Right Fruit. *The Scientist* 12 (August 17). www.the-scientist.library.upenn.edu/yr1998/August/pg4_story2_980817.html. Visited January 7, 2000.

Smillie, W. 1952. The Period of Great Epidemics in the United States (1800–1875). In *The History of American Epidemiology* Edited by R. H. Top. St. Louis: C. V. Mosby, pp. 52–73.

Smith, A. G. 2000. How Toxic is DDT? *Lancet* 356, 267–68.

Smith, Andrew G. 1991. Chlorinated Hydrocarbon Insecticides. In *Handbook of Pesticide Toxicology*. Edited by Wayland J. Hayes Jr. and Edward R. Laws Jr. San Diego: Academic Press, pp. 731–915.

Smith, Daniel. 1999. Worldwide Trends in DDT Levels in Human Breast Milk. *International Journal of Epidemiology* 28, no. 2, 179–88.

Smith, Frances B. 2000. The Biosafety Protocol: The Real Losers Are Developing Countries. *BRIEFLY. . .Perspectives on Legislation, Regulation and Litigation* 4, no. 3 (March). Washington: National Legal Center for the Public Interest.

Stone, Christopher D. 2001. Is There a Precautionary Principle? *Environmental Law Reporter*. Forthcoming.

Swaminathan, M. S. 1999. Genetic Engineering and Food, Ecological and Livelihood Security in Predominantly Agricultural Developing Countries. Paper presented at CGIAR/NAS Biotechnology Conference, October 21–22, Washington, D.C. www.cgiar.org/biotechc/swami.htm. Visited November 11, 1999.

Tabashnik, Bruce E., et al. 2000. Frequency of Resistance to *Bacillus thuringiensis* in Field Populations of Pink Bollworm. *Proceedings of the National Academy of Sciences* 97, no. 24, 12,980–84.

Tans, P. P., and J. W. C. White. 1998. The Global Carbon Cycle: In Balance, with a Little Help from the Plants. *Science* 281, 183–84.

Taubes, G. 1997. Global Warming: Apocalypse Not. *Science* 278, 1004–06.

Taylor, Terrie E., and Irving F. Hoffman. 2000. Can HIV-1 Infections in Africa Provide Insights into Acquired Immunity to Malaria? *Lancet* 356, 1046.

Tian, H., et al. 1998. Effect of Interannual Climate Variability on Carbon Storage in Amazonian Ecosystems. *Nature* 396, 664–67.

Tickner, Joel A. 1999. A Map toward Precautionary Decision Making. In *Protecting Public Health and the Environment: Implementing the Precautionary Principle*. Edited by Carolyn Raffensperger and Joel Tickner. Washington: Island Press, pp. 162–86.

Tolkien, J. R. R. 1937. *The Hobbit*. New York: Ballantine, revised edition (1985).

Tren, Richard, and Roger Bate. 2001. *Malaria and the DDT Story*. London: Institute of Economic Affairs.

United Nations. 1974. *Universal Declaration on the Eradication of Hunger and Malnutrition*. www.unhchr.ch/html/intlinst.htm. Visited April 14, 2001.

_____. 1992. *AGENDA 21: The UN Programme of Action from Rio*. New York: United Nations.

_____. 1998. *Fiftieth Anniversary of the Universal Declaration of Human Rights, 1948–1998*. Available at www.un.org/Overview/rights.html. Visited April 14, 2001.

_____. 1999. *Declaration on the Right and Responsibility of Individuals, Groups and Organs of Society to Promote and Protect Universally Recognized Human Rights and Fundamental Freedoms*. General Assembly Resolution 53/144. March 8.

United Nations Development Program. 1999. *Human Development Report 1999*. New York: Oxford University Press.

United Nations Environment Program. 2000. *Report of the Intergovernmental Negotiating Committee for an International Legally Binding Instrument for Implementing International Action on Certain Persistent Organic Pollutants on the Work of Its Fifth Session*. UNEP/POPS/INC.5/7. 26 December.

United Nations Environment Program/Global Environmental Monitoring System. 1991. *Environmental Data Report 1991–92*. Cambridge: Blackwell.

United Nations Framework Convention on Climate Change. 1992. *UN Framework Convention on Climate Change*. www.unfccc.de.

United Nations Population Division. 1999. *Long-Range World Population Projections: Based on the 1998 Revision*. Report ESA/P/WP.153. New York: United Nations.

United States Bureau of Commerce. 1987. *Statistical Abstract of the United States*. Washington: Government Printing Office.

Vogt, Donna U. 1995. *The Delaney Clause Effects on Pesticide Policy*. Congressional Research Service: Report for Congress. Available from the Committee for the National Institute for the Environment at www.cnie.org/nle/pest-1.html. Visited April 3, 2001.

Waggoner, Paul E. 1994. *How Much Land Can Ten Billion People Spare for Nature?* Ames, Iowa: Council for Agricultural Science and Technology.

Walliman, T. 2000. *Bt* Toxin: Assessing GM Strategies. *Science* 287, 41.

Warrick, J. 1998. Reassessing Kyoto Agreement, Scientists See Little Environmental Advantage. *Washington Post*, February 13: A14.

Warrick, R. A., et al. 1996. Changes in Sea Level. In IPCC. 1996b. *Climate Change 1995: The Science of Climate Change*. Cambridge: Cambridge University Press, pp. 359–405.

Whelan, Elizabeth M. 1992. *Toxic Terror: The Truth behind the Cancer Scares*. Buffalo, N.Y: Prometheus Books.

Whitworth, James, et al. 2000. Effect of HIV-1 and Increasing Immunosuppression on Malaria Parasitaemia and Clinical Episodes in Adults in Rural Uganda: A Cohort Study. *Lancet* 356, 1051–56.

Wigley, T. M. L. 1997. Implications of Recent CO_2 Emission-Limitation Proposals for Stabilization of Atmospheric Concentrations. *Nature* 390, 267–70.

_____. 1998. The Kyoto Protocol: CO_2, CH_4 and Climate Implications. *Geophysical Research Letters* 25, 2285–88.

Wigley, T. M. L., et al. 1996. Economic and Environmental Choices in the Stabilization of Atmospheric CO2 Concentrations. *Nature* 379, 240–43.

Wilcove, D. S., et al. 1998. Quantifying Threats to Imperiled Species in the United States. *BioScience* 48, 607–15.

Williams, Jonathan. 1998. Organic Farming in the Uplands of Mid Wales. Statement at Earth Options, Second "Look Out Wales" Environmental Forum, May 1998. www.wyeside.co.uk/expotec/earth_options /htm. Visited March 19, 2000.

Wittwer, Sylvan H. 1995. *Food, Climate and Carbon Dioxide: The Global Environment and World Food Production*. Boca Raton, Fla.: Lewis Publishers, pp. 56–57.

World Bank. 1992. *Global Economic Prospects and the Developing Countries*. Washington: World Bank.

_____. 1993. *World Development Report 1993: Investing in Health*. New York: Oxford University Press.

_____. *New & Noteworthy in Nutrition*. Issue 24. www.worldbank.org/html/extdr/ hnp/nutrition/nnn/nnn24.htm. Visited January 5, 2000.

References

_____. 1999. *World Development Indicators*. CD-ROM. Washington: World Bank.

_____. 2000. *World Development Report 2000/2001: Attacking Poverty*. New York: Oxford University Press.

World Climate Report. 2001. Satellite "Warming" Vanishes. Vol 6, no. 9.

World Health Organization. 1997. *Health and Environment in Sustainable Development*. Fact Sheet No. 170. Geneva: World Health Organization.

_____. 1999a. *The World Health Report 1999*. Geneva: World Health Organization.

_____. 1999b. *About WHO: Nutrition*. September 21. www.who.int/aboutwho/en/promoting/nutrition.htm. Visited January 5, 2000.

_____. 1999c. *Malnutrition Worldwide*. November 22, 1999. www.who.int/nut/malnutrition_worldwide.htm. Visited January 5, 2000.

_____. 2000. *The World Health Report 2000*. Geneva: World Health Organization.

World Resources Institute. 1998. *World Resources 1998–99 Database*. Washington: World Resources Institute.

World Wildlife Fund. 1999. *Persistent Organic Pollutants: Hand-Me-Down Poisons That Threaten Wildlife and People*. Issue Brief. Washington: World Wildlife Fund.

_____. 2001. *WWF's Efforts to Phase Out DDT*. Available at www.worldwildlife.org/toxics/progareas/pop/ddt.htm. Visited 14 April 2001.

Wraight, C. L., A. R. Zangerl, M. J. Carroll, and M. R. Berenbaum. 2000. Absence of Toxicity of *Bacillus thuringiensis* Pollen to Black Swallowtails under Field Conditions. *Proceedings of the National Academy of Sciences* 97, 7700–03.

Ye, Xudong, et al. 2000. Engineering the Provitamin A (â-Carotene) Biosynthetic Pathway into (Carotenoid-Free) Rice Endosperm. *Science* 287, 303–05.

Zhang, Q. 1999. *Meeting the Challenges of Food Production: The Opportunities of Agricultural Biotechnology in China*. Paper presented at CGIAR/NAS Biotechnology Conference, October 21–22, Washington, D.C. www.cgiar.org/biotechc/zhang.htm. Visited November 11, 1999.

Zucker, Jane R. 1996. Changing Patterns of Autochthonous Malaria Transmission in the United States: A Review of Recent Outbreaks. *Emerging Infectious Diseases* 2, 37–43.

Index

Massachusetts Institute of Technology (MIT) Joint Program on the Science and Technology of Global Change, 74
Meat, protein-enhanced GM crops leading to reduction in need for, 40
Melons, reduction in spoilage-proneness of, 35
Metabolites of DDT, 14, 19, 21
Metal absorption by GM crops, 37
Methyl mercury detoxification by GM crops, 37
Migrations, animal and plant, 63
Milk (human), DDT detected in, 1, 13, 14, 18, 19–20
MIT (Massachusetts Institute of Technology) Joint Program on the Science and Technology of Global Change, 74
Monarch butterfly larvae affected by *Bt* plants, 42–43
Mortality/life expectancy
  affluence, diseases of, 40, 48, 49
  crude death rate (CDR), global drop in, 64
  economic growth and development and , 22–25, 75
  extreme temperatures, effect on human health of, 65, 79–80
  extreme weather events, effect of, 69
  GM crops and, 38–41, 50
  human capital, investment in, 24
  human mortality/morbidity criterion. *See* Public health criterion
  malaria and, 13, 15, 17–18, 20
  malaria, WHO estimate of cost of reducing death rate from, 74
  New Orleans, in 19th century, 64
  technological improvements and, 3
  vector-borne diseases and global warming, 64
Mosquitoes
  Anopheles species, 15, 16, 63
  diseases other than malaria borne by, DDT preventing, 18
  global warming and, 63
  resistance to DDT and other pesticides, 13, 15, 16, 21–22, 89
  toxicity of DDT, species of mosquitoes affected by, 15, 16
  See also DDT (dichlorodiphenyltrichloro-ethane); Malaria

Mothers' milk, DDT detected in, 1, 13, 14, 18, 19–20
Moths, *Bt* plants' effect on, 43
Mueller, Paul, 13
Munitions dumps, biodegradation of, 41
Mycotoxins, GM crops with lower levels of, 41
Mymensingh (Bangladesh), 22, 50

National Ambient Air Quality Standards, 4
Nepal, 16
Nitrogen
  rice capable of fixing, 34, 36
  uptake from soil, 34, 36
  see also Nutrients in the environment
Nitrous oxide reductions, 36, 84
"No regrets" actions, 57
Nobel Prizes
  Haber's process to synthesize ammonia, 34
  Mueller's research on malaria, 13
North Atlantic, thermohaline circulation of, 59
North Korea, 17
North Sea, Second and Third International Conferences on the Protection of, 4
Norwalk virus, 40
Novartis, 48
Nuclear power, 94
Nutrients in the environment, 29, 36–37, 51
Nutritional issues. *See* Food supply, undernourishment, and malnutrition

Oceans
  iron fertilization of, 88, 94
  sea level rise (SLR), 63, 67, 68
  thermohaline circulation of North Atlantic, 59
Oils and oil products produced from GM crops, 35, 40
Ospreys, DDT's effect on, 1, 13, 21

Papaya, disease- and insect-resistant, 34–35
Paper, GM trees used in making, 38
Paraguay, 17
Paratyphoid, 64
Peanuts, GM varieties of, 40
Peregrine falcons, DDT's effect on, 1, 13, 21

About the Author

Indur M. Goklany is an independent scholar with over 25 years of experience working on global warming, biotechnology, biodiversity, and other environmental issues at various levels of state and federal government, as well as in the private sector. He serves as a manager in the Department of the Interior's Office of Policy Analysis. He has represented the United States at the Intergovernmental Panel on Climate Change (IPCC) and in the negotiations that established the UN Framework Convention on Climate Change. He previously served as chief of the Technical Assessment Division of the National Commission on Air Quality and as a consultant to the Environmental Protection Agency's Office of Policy, Planning, and Evaluation. He is the author of *Clearing the Air: The Real Story about the War on Air Pollution.* He lives in the Washington, D.C., area with his wife and family.

Cato Institute

Founded in 1977, the Cato Institute is a public policy research foundation dedicated to broadening the parameters of policy debate to allow consideration of more options that are consistent with the traditional American principles of limited government, individual liberty, and peace. To that end, the Institute strives to achieve greater involvement of the intelligent, concerned lay public in questions of policy and the proper role of government.

The Institute is named for *Cato's Letters*, libertarian pamphlets that were widely read in the American Colonies in the early 18th century and played a major role in laying the philosophical foundation for the American Revolution.

Despite the achievement of the nation's Founders, today virtually no aspect of life is free from government encroachment. A pervasive intolerance for individual rights is shown by government's arbitrary intrusions into private economic transactions and its disregard for civil liberties.

To counter that trend, the Cato Institute undertakes an extensive publications program that addresses the complete spectrum of policy issues. Books, monographs, and shorter studies are commissioned to examine the federal budget, Social Security, regulation, military spending, international trade, and myriad other issues. Major policy conferences are held throughout the year, from which papers are published thrice yearly in the *Cato Journal*. The Institute also publishes the quarterly magazine *Regulation*.

In order to maintain its independence, the Cato Institute accepts no government funding. Contributions are received from foundations, corporations, and individuals, and other revenue is generated from the sale of publications. The Institute is a nonprofit, tax-exempt, educational foundation under Section 501(c)3 of the Internal Revenue Code.

CATO INSTITUTE
1000 Massachusetts Ave., N.W.
Washington, D.C. 20001